RYAN SERHANT

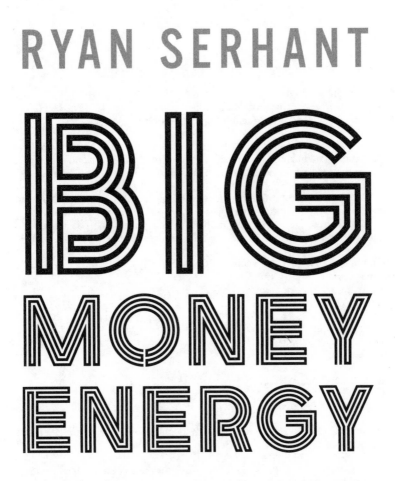

BIG MONEY ENERGY

HOW TO **RULE AT WORK,** **DOMINATE AT LIFE,** AND **MAKE MILLIONS**

hachette
BOOKS

NEW YORK

Hachette Go, an imprint of Hachette Books
Hachette Book Group
1290 Avenue of the Americas
New York, NY 10104

HachetteGo.com
Facebook.com/HachetteGo
Instagram.com/HachetteGo

First Edition: January 2021

Hachette Books is a division of Hachette Book Group, Inc.

The Hachette Go and Hachette Books name and logos are trademarks of
Hachette Book Group, Inc.

The publisher is not responsible for websites (or their content) that are not
owned by the publisher.

Editorial production by Christine Marra, *Marra*thon Production Services.
www.marrathoneditorial.org

Book design by Jane Raese
Set in 11-point Linoletter

Library of Congress Control Number: 2020946664

ISBNs: 978-0-306-92310-4 (hardcover); 978-0-306-92470-5 (B&N Signed
Edition) 978-0-306-92311-1 (ebook)

Printed in the United States of America

LSC-C

Printing 1, 2020

This book is dedicated to my daughter.

Zena, you give me the energy to go bigger every day.

And to my amazing team at SERHANT.,

who helped me build our new company, during a pandemic,

while I was busy writing this book.

AUTHOR'S NOTE

I have changed the names as well as some identifying details throughout the book. I'd also like to add that while it's been over a decade since my first sale, I can still remember the addresses of every single apartment I've ever sold. However, I cannot say that I can remember all of the details about conversations I've had with people. I've made an attempt to recapture these conversations to the extent that my memory allows.

CONTENTS

WHAT IS BIG MONEY ENERGY?

You're reading this book because there's something that you *want* that you don't have.

It could be your dream job, more money, an affluent lifestyle, or the self-confidence to move through the world with ease, knowing you have the power to get whatever you want along the way.

I know exactly what it feels like to want a bigger and better life. Just ten years ago, I was living commission check to commission check. Barely making ends meet, stuck in survival mode. Yet everywhere I looked I'd see people who just exuded success. Accomplishment and confidence oozed from their pores like some sort of magical, liquid gold. It was evident in the way they walked, talked, dressed, and smiled. To be clear, I'm not talking about the obvious signs of status. I didn't think I could just throw on a fancy watch (which I would have had to steal anyway) and automatically change my entire life. But I wanted to be like the ultra-confident people who were walking down the street beside me. I wanted my fear of failure to stop ruling my life.

I wanted to break through all the constant obstacles thrown in my path. Clearly these put-together, confident-looking people were on their way to important meetings with captains of industry or power lunches—I wanted to be THAT! I wanted Big Money Energy.

Big Money Energy is the vibe you get from someone who is massively succeeding at life in every direction. You know this person. You notice him or her instantly when they walk by in the office, because their confidence is glowing like a halo, *but humbly*. Or you see this person at a party and her energy is so big that she effortlessly stands out in the crowd.

A person with Big Money Energy is the ultimate picture of self-confidence. There's no bravado—no bragging—they know they have BME and so does everyone else. It's completely obvious. People who possess Big Money Energy get that way because they are 100% committed to making their vision for themselves a reality, and their vision is BIG.

When you meet someone with BME you can't help but want to be around them. They're confident, but never cocky. They understand the path to success is paved with hard work, gratitude, patience, and experience. This person has learned to brush loss off her shoulders. She stays determined and keeps her eye on the prize ahead.

People with BME never stop learning, earning, and growing.

If you want more for yourself, but bigger and better feels out of reach, know that it's not—it's ALL yours for the taking!

(And if you think you've already maximized your potential, then by all means enjoy floating around in your gold-plated infinity pool. Just have your butler toss this book in the volcano that came along with your private island because, clearly, you've figured it all out and you don't need any help from me at all.)*

In 2008 my annual earnings were $9,188. After designing a whole new Ryan, and going BIGGER, ten years later I am earning a million dollars every month! I've managed to build a blueprint for unshakeable BME. I've outlined it for you in this book, along with stories from my own life so you can see how BME completely changed the course of my career, and I've also sprinkled in codes and the tools I've used to bring greater success into my life every day. People aren't born with Big Money Energy (well most of us aren't; I know I wasn't) and it's not an energy that's exclusive to celebrities, the wealthy, the freakishly good looking, the well connected, and the powerful. It lives inside all of us. This book will show you how to unleash your Big Money Energy so that you can achieve more financial growth for yourself, succeed on levels greater than you ever expected, and expand your dreams to outrageous proportions. I want you to want more for yourself!

In the following pages I am going to guide you through the same process that I used to transform myself into the guy who makes more money than I ever imagined by the time I turned thirty-five. As a former low-rent salesman who woke up every morning worried about how I would

---

*Will you please email me and tell me how you did it? Islands with volcanoes must be very expensive. My email address is Ryan@RyanSerhant.com.

succeed, I know it can all be turned around if you follow the steps I'm going to lay out in the chapters ahead.

And guess what? I know you have Big Money Energy inside of you, and I am determined to help you unleash it. I want to make you the best version of yourself—the one you've always imagined you can be. I want you to wake up every day excited to live another day as YOU, and to know that you can achieve any vision you create for yourself, no matter how massive it is. So, if you want to be where you WANT to be, and not just where you are, then let's GO.

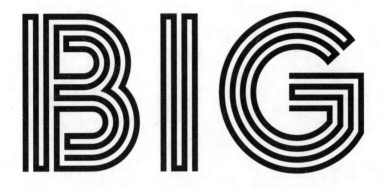

There's no way you're going to accept an average, run-of-the-mill kind of life. You don't have to. You want massive success. Your vision for your life is huge. You're going to crush your goals and take everything you do to extraordinary new heights. Bigger isn't just better, it's everything.

CHAPTER 1

GO BIGGER

When I answered the phone in my office on a random Tuesday morning in 2009, I thought it would either be a broker calling to scream at me because another one of my clients had just pulled out of a deal, or the usual "Hi. I'm looking for a cheap two-bedroom apartment that me and my six best friends can be stuffed into." But before I could start reeling off information about listings, the woman on the phone shared that her name was June Shen. She worked for a large oil and gas company in China, and she was looking to buy an apartment in New York. This was, to say the least, unexpected. I had never sold an apartment to someone from another country before.

"Okay, that's . . . GREAT!" I said. "What are you looking for exactly and what's your budget?"

"$2 million or so, but if we need to spend more, we can." Chills went up my spine. My jaw didn't just hit the floor—I swear it detached from my face and floated down gently in a cloud of sparkles. $2 million? In the middle of a recession while everyone is losing their jobs?

I had done some small sales under $1 million in the first half of 2009, but nothing this big before. Then I asked her another genius question: "When do you plan on moving to New York City?"

"Oh, we would never do that. This is just an investment for my daughter."

"How old is your daughter?"

"Oh, she's not born yet. But she will be soon." Wait. What? She was buying an apartment for a baby . . . who wasn't even born yet? "So, Ryan, I'll be in town for a couple of days later in the month. Can you help me out by showing me some apartments?"

While I was tempted to say, "I'd love to help you, but I've never sold a seven-figure apartment before and I have no idea what I'm doing," I responded with "Oh YEAH, I can help you find the *perfect* apartment because it's what I was *BORN to do*."* Oh my God. Then I hung up the phone and started to panic.

The reality was that I was a brand new real estate agent in Manhattan, living a very hand-to-mouth, commission-check-to-rent existence in one of the most expensive and intensely competitive cities in the world. And I was really struggling. I'd wake up every day and think, Oh, it's morning. Hello, anxiety. How are you doing this fine day? What's going on, dread? You hanging in there, li'l buddy? And then I'd go about my day, acting like I had my own personal storm cloud following me around everywhere I went. This wasn't what I wanted—I craved success.

But I had convinced myself that success was reserved for other people. Success was the domain of those who were

---

*That is literally what I said, word for word. Remembering this makes me cringe!

more confident, better educated, well connected, smarter, richer, better looking, bolder.

It felt like everyone was raking in the big bucks but me. At work, other realtors were getting clients with much larger budgets, while I was stuck with clients looking to live life on the cheap, living in fear of a negative bank balance just like I was.

My constant worry was about money. In fact, it consumed me. Before I spent even one dollar on anything—a sandwich, subway ride, bar of soap, pair of socks, or new toothbrush—I had to ask myself, *If I buy this item will I still have enough left over to pay my rent?* Every dollar was accounted for, and there were never enough of them. I was tired of being the guy my lawyer and finance friends bought drinks for out of pity. I wanted to be the guy who said, "I'll get this round!" instead of nursing a seltzer I pretended was vodka, because that's all I could afford.

I knew I was never going to get out of this cycle if I kept renting out studios and out-of-the-way one-bedroom apartments. I was sick of waking up and going to bed worried about money. The worry felt like a pain in my side—it never left me.

But the problem was, I didn't even want to do business with myself!

Nothing about me said, "Let me help you spend millions of dollars." I didn't even own a suit! I felt low rent, looked low rent, and acted low rent. Why would June Shen want to buy a fancy apartment from someone like me, who was dripping with desperation? I'd been living like that for years, and if I didn't make some serious changes, I knew I could look forward to living the same unsatisfying life forever.

That day, as I looked at my closet and contemplated how many times I had worn the exact same button-down shirt to meet clients, I realized that June Shen knew nothing about me other than my name was Ryan and I was a real estate agent in New York. She didn't know that I looked like the kid who got picked last in gym, or that I had never sold a multimillion-dollar apartment, ever. She had found me on the internet because of an open listing I had posted, and she called me by chance, at random. For all June knew, I could be rolling around in a giant pile of $1,000 bills while I was talking to her. This was an opportunity to present myself in the way I wanted to be seen. This was a chance to wipe the slate clean. June needed to meet the bigger version of Ryan, the person I had often dreamed about becoming while lying in my studio apartment, the one without a bathroom. That bigger Ryan was confident, energetic, and closed deals for breakfast. I wanted June Shen to meet me as that guy, someone who was already successful, not some kid.

I started thinking about the picture of success I wanted to present to June. I had to be brutally honest with myself. My fifth-year-college-student look wasn't going to cut it. I dug out my Macy's credit card (that I had never used) and purchased the nicest-looking suit I could afford.

Taking the subway wasn't going to send the right signal either. The successful brokers in my office took their clients around in town cars. I googled "limo service New York City," clicked on the first link, and rented a black SUV that looked very well used but came with a driver to take us around. (Nowadays there's Uber!)

My credit card was seeing a lot of action. With a new suit and a black car booked, I decided that I'd be the master of

New York streets. I went crazy studying everything about the blocks of New York before June's arrival. It was intense, like I was studying to take the LSAT! I studied street names, business locations, tourist sites, you name it.

The deals I had made thus far as a new agent had been generally limited to Murray Hill and the Village and the outer boroughs—I had barely even set foot in the nicer parts of town where the apartments were more expensive and appealed to more affluent people.

But I had to seem knowledgeable, and without hesitation. She needed to know that I really knew what I was doing, but I didn't know what I was doing. I didn't know what clients usually asked before buying an apartment that cost millions of dollars, so I also memorized every fact about each building I was going to show her: when it was built, the architect who designed it, the developer on the project, and who else lived there. For weeks I forced myself to learn and be prepared for *any* question June might ask me. I researched the land the buildings were built on so that I could give her some history about Manhattan. If a celebrity lived in a building we were looking at, I knew about it. If a scene from a movie was shot there, I knew all the details. I took note of all the playgrounds so I could point out the places where little June junior could play. At one point I really needed a snack so I stopped in a coffee shop. I noticed the guy who was working there was named Bob. I thought, Wow. If I bring June here for a coffee and I know Bob by name it will seem like I'm in this expensive neighborhood all the time! I'll appear like a big-time agent just by association!

I woke up the day of my appointment with June feeling ready to go, though I had barely slept since I was so nervous. The SUV picked me up at my apartment in Korea-town, and as we drove uptown to June's hotel, sitting in the back seat, being driven to a multimillion-dollar client, I realized that I was experiencing a level of calm and confidence I had never felt before. The nerves from last night were gone. For once, I was going to meet a potential buyer, filled with positive energy. Remarkably, I didn't feel afraid of falling flat on my face.

When we pulled up to the corner where her hotel was, I noticed a very exhausted and very pregnant Chinese woman standing there in a baggy, wrinkled track suit. I rolled down the window, feeling just a little bit like Richard Gere in *Pretty Woman*. "June? Hi! I'm Ryan!"

June weakly lifted up a hand to indicate that, yes, it was her. I got out to open the car door for her, she slid in, leaned against the door, and immediately fell asleep. Oh, okay, well—the flight from China is really long.

We spent the next couple of days following the same pattern: I'd pick up June, she'd get in the car and take a nap. I'd wake her up when we got to the property we were looking at and she would get out and walk around the apartment in total silence. Oh my God, is she sleepwalking? What do I do? You're never supposed to wake up a sleep-walker, right? But then we'd get back to the car, and she'd say, "I don't like it" (so she was awake!) and immediately fall back to sleep.

The afternoon of her last day in the city it was very hot and humid. We still hadn't found the perfect apartment for her unborn child, and I'd racked up so many charges on my credit card I had no idea how I would pay them off. June needed a drink and a snack, so we got hot dogs and bottled water from a street cart, and we headed to the Rushmore, a brand new condominium building developed by Extell at 80 Riverside Boulevard. It was gorgeous. This was the opposite of what showing walk-up convertible three-beds with no A/C in Astoria, Queens, feels like. This felt GREAT. This felt right. This felt like my future, and I was living it.

June woke back up when the car pulled over, her half-eaten hot dog still in her hand. When we got inside the apartment, everything was different. Suddenly June Shen was wide awake—and she broke her silence! "I like this!" *Yesssss.* We started looking at the kitchen, and then the bathrooms, and by the time we got to the bedroom where someday her baby would sleep she said, "This is the one, let's make an offer." We got back in the car and June went right back to sleep while I bounced up and down, grinning from ear to ear—I was about to sell an apartment with an asking price of $2.5 million to a fetus! I. WAS. GOING. TO. BE. RICH!!

————————

Fast-forward a few nights later, and after my first major negotiation with a developer, I'm standing in the lobby of the St. Regis Hotel at 3 A.M. The big greasy bag of cheeseburgers that a still very jet-lagged June requested I bring her was overpowering the lobby's carefully cultivated scent of wealth and power. But I had done it! I had negotiated like I had been doing this for ten years, knocked $300,000 off the price, and sold June's unborn child a $2.2 million apartment at 80 Riverside Boulevard. June was ready to sign the contract while inhaling curly fries.

I had managed to close a really, really big deal in the middle of a recession. It was a preview of what life could look like if I let go of my low-money mindset. Nothing else had changed in my life: I was still just a young real estate agent with no contacts. But while nothing really *changed*, everything did.

My parents came to visit me a few months later, just after the closing. I met my dad outside of his hotel before dinner and asked him to walk with me to the bank. I bank with Chase, and it can feel like they have ATMs on every corner of the city, which is great when you have checks to deposit, but bad when you don't and they just remind you of all the money you don't have. But for the first time ever (!!!), I was going to the ATM because I had a massive $24,000 commission check burning a hole in my coat pocket.

My dad stood next to me as I watched my bank balance shoot from a few hundred dollars to nearly $25,000. I couldn't believe it. This was the most money I had ever seen in my bank account! My dad was proud, but I could tell he wasn't as impressed as I was. To me, this achievement represented a massive, life-altering win. In my mind this was as good as it gets, and I was going to soak up every ounce of enjoyment from the experience. This money would cover rent for the next two years of my life! I could buy new shoes, I could go grocery shopping!!! Hell, I could even be Mr. Generous and replace the shower curtain in the bathroom I shared with twenty-five other people.

"You think this is really something?" Dad asked. Heck yeah, I did. "It's nice, bud, but you need to understand there is much more where this came from. Just look around. The world is full of June Shens. There are nearly 10 million of them in this city alone. They just don't know you yet."

Sure, $24,000 was a lot of money (especially when you had none), but what if my dad was right? What if at this exact moment, I wasn't at the top of my game? What if this check was just the first step towards something much, much bigger? The more I thought about it, the more it made sense. Not having to worry about rent was a huge relief. But only working to make rent meant that I was just surviving, and I wanted to do more than that—I wanted to thrive! I wanted more for myself than a handful of rent payments. I wanted it ALL. I'll never forget standing there at that ATM with my dad and wondering how far I could *really* go.

GO BIG OR GO HOME

That khaki-clad, overly anxious kid who didn't believe he'd ever be on the winning side of the game had finally scored, for once. And when I thought about it, I was still the same semi-anxious guy, but the little changes I had started to make inside made a difference. The truth was, not all that much about me had changed. I hadn't undergone a drastic makeover. A new suit and a driver helped me feel more confident, but I realized that the secret sauce was how it enabled me to control my energy, and THAT is what needed to change to become the power broker I wanted to be. Instead of dripping desperation, I was able to exude the energy of a knowledgeable, capable, and confident businessman. I learned a very life-altering lesson that was the first stop in understanding how to manifest BIG success. I couldn't change how much money I had in the bank or what kinds of clothes I could afford—but I could change my *presence,* I could work on how I came off to people.

CODE #1

When you can't change your circumstances, there's one thing you can change: your energy.

The energy you give out comes from the core of who you are as a person. Your energy can come off to others as influential and powerful, or timid and insignificant. I was a low-energy ball of sadness who picked up equally sad people wherever I went. If I was riding the subway, I'd inevitably end up sitting next to the saddest person in the world who would tell me all about her recent breakup with her boyfriend. If I was standing in line to buy a salad, it was almost guaranteed that the person behind me in line would open up about how they just got fired by THEIR JERK BOSS AND LIFE SUCKS AND UGH I HATE EVERYONE. Misery loves company, and so does bad energy. If you're low energy all day, you'll attract other low-energy work and clients. If you put negative energy out into the world, you'll surround yourself with abuse because subconsciously that's what you're asking for. At the office, the positive, energetic people would go out for drinks after work sometimes. I'd watch them walk out of the office, smiling and laughing together like life was a grand party. I'd be left behind with Tim who was so low energy and so quiet he practically blended into

16

the wall, and Harry whose main job in life was complaining about everything. This was not the club I wanted to belong to! I wanted to be happy like those other guys, but I felt like I didn't fit in with them because they made a lot more money than me.

Selling that apartment to June was the first time I understood that when you control your energy and hold yourself to a higher standard, anything becomes possible. No matter how big and how bold, nothing will be out of reach for you, because changing your energy means winning the game and putting losing behind you forever. And I know it's possible, because I did it. During the height of my struggles as a new real estate broker in New York City, I was essentially "Ryan Serhant, poster boy for how not to succeed at life." I was desperate when I wanted to be confident, unsure when I wanted to be certain, slouching because I was too afraid to stand tall, and quiet when I should have spoken up. I knew I wanted to leave low-rent Ryan behind forever, but how would I get started?

The way I imagined big success as a kid growing up on a farm outside of Boston was lots of money in the bank, a closetful of suits, a fast car, and a sleek apartment, and who knows what else—was that even a possibility for me?

After my experience with June Shen I realized that I had two choices: give up on myself or realize that I was a blank canvas that could be worked on. I was now going to be very deliberate about how I moved forward. I didn't want to wait to start living bigger, and I didn't want to depend on anyone else to give me that permission either. I wanted my power back—the power I lost somewhere along the way in my search for success. I wanted the power I was born with but had lost to social pressures and crippling anxiety. I was done holding back. I had made just one bold stroke, and my canvas already looked better! I was going to do whatever it took to transform the canvas of my life into something priceless. It wasn't easy—I didn't snap my fingers and watch self-conscious and broke Ryan fade into the distance. It took a lot of work, self-evaluation, and practice. As I started to let myself have greater expectations about what I was capable of, the more I accomplished, the more my career started to grow.

Examine the picture of your life right now—is it what you want? *Really*, is it? We've all had something we fantasized about doing, but we let fear hold us back. Or maybe someone told us our dreams were stupid. *Being a magician isn't a real career! Are you insane?* It's easy to talk yourself out of pursuing a dream if you're worried about screwing up, going broke, or looking like a total idiot. *The show was pretty good until the magician tried to saw that lady in half— my kids will be traumatized forever.* What if your biggest desires could be a reality? What if you couldn't screw up? Change your energy and the picture of your life will look entirely different. Right now it might be messy and chaotic, or too tidy and predictable. If you commit to thinking bigger, taking bigger actions, dreaming bigger, and opening your mind up to every crazy possibility, you can LIVE BIG.

CHAPTER 2

BE THE FUTURE YOU RIGHT NOW

ARE YOU A TOP-LEVEL REAL ESTATE BROKER
WHO WANTS TO BE ON TV?

Description: Casting real estate brokers in New York City for unscripted television show. Are you a successful real estate broker selling high-end real estate in Manhattan? Bravo TV is holding auditions for a New York City based version of Million Dollar Listing. Click here to apply.

The ad on Curbed.com caught my eye right away. At that point in my life I wasn't exactly a "top level" real estate broker, but I had started selling more apartments after meeting June, and a few of them were in the seven-figure range. I was definitely moving up in the world. I was now focused on my real estate career, but that was a relatively new decision. The whole reason I came to New York in the first place was to be an actor! I had spent the last two years of my life auditioning for television shows, plays, and commercials, and made very little money doing it. In fact, there was little to show for any of that time of my life, other than a brief appearance as an evil doctor on a soap opera and roles in some off-off-off-off-Broadway plays. Oh, and I was a hand model, as some of you may remember from *Sell It Like Serhant.* Yep—a professional one. I was paid to hold phones while the director yelled at me for not bending the metatarsal on my right ring finger seven degrees forward. My passion was to act. I had saved up as much money as I could and gave myself two years to give it a go in the toughest city in the world. What could go wrong?! Obviously I didn't know what I was getting myself into. It turns out you need a lot of money to live in Manhattan, and playing the role of a tree in a basement production of *Macbeth* didn't pay too well. If I wanted more to life than constant stress about money, I had to face the fact that my acting career wasn't going to cut it, so I got my real estate license to help pay the bills. I thought it would just be a survival job—a job that brought in enough to pay the bills while I worked towards making it on Broadway or landing a role in a movie. But then something surprising happened: I really started to like the business. I liked being a salesperson! The rejection wasn't nearly as bad in sales as it felt at auditions. I didn't take it personally if someone didn't like an apartment. I also felt a thrill every time I closed a deal. It was satisfying to connect a person to something they wanted, and *actually get paid to do it.*

I figured the *Million Dollar Listing* opportunity, which combined television (my quickly fading dream) and real estate (which was turning out to be an area where I was really starting to shine), was a great way to take my career to a higher level.

I mean, at the very least I would have a better chance than most brokers. How many real estate brokers had acting training? It's like this opportunity was meant for me!

I filled out the very short application that entailed writing down my name and email address (they were being *really* selective) and received a quick response:

Dear Top Real Estate Broker:
>Thank you for applying to be on Million Dollar Listing: New York!
>Report to the Hudson Hotel at 356 W 58th St, New York, NY 10019.
>Your scheduled interview time is: **1:30 p.m. on Wednesday, March 10th, 2010.**
>We look forward to meeting you!

My Macy's suit was fresh from the cleaners, and I put on my best shirt and a new tie. I made sure my shoes were extra polished, and thankfully my hair was having a good day. I felt great! When I reported to the Hudson Hotel at my appointed time, it quickly became clear that not only did New York City have an unlimited supply of wannabe actors, it also had an unlimited supply of real estate brokers who wanted to be on TV. *Awesome!*

The lobby of the Hudson Hotel is dark and moody with a quiet and sophisticated vibe. But that day it was packed from end to end with real estate brokers who were all trying out for the same job as me. *Why exactly did I think this was a good idea?* I went from feeling like Superman to Bizarro.*

---

*FYI, Bizarro is a DC Comics character who is the exact opposite of Superman. Now you know.

I sat down on a plush velvet couch, my self-esteem sinking deeper into it with each thought. I was selling more, and I was finally getting comfortable in my career. My inner-Superman was cheering me on: "You are a great broker, Ryan! This opportunity is perfect for you! Go get it!" But then my inner-Bizzaro said: "Why are you back at an audition?" Then he laughed (maniacally), because auditions went so well the first time?! "The world of film and television didn't want you before, why would they want you now?"

I had talked to my friend David about it. He didn't hide the fact that he thought it was an idiotic idea: "Really, Ryan? How will being on a stupid reality TV show be good for your business? I wouldn't hire a lawyer from a TV show—why would someone hire a *television real estate broker*?" he said with a grossed-out expression.

My mom's reaction wasn't much better. After a long sigh, I could practically hear her eyes roll through the phone. "Who will take you seriously if you're running around town selling real estate on television? I wouldn't hire someone from *Survivor* to sell our home. You will make a joke of yourself," she said.

All of my insecurities were resurfacing, and the longer I waited, the larger my doubt grew. My inner monologue went like this:

Who am I kidding? I'm not a top broker. That's a joke. I've only been in real estate for a year and a half! Just a couple of years ago I was sharing a bathroom with a dozen other people. I just moved into a legit studio apartment (with its own bathroom!), but I don't have the cash to buy furniture! WHAT KIND OF TOP REAL ESTATE BROKER EATS DINNER WHILE SITTING ON THE FLOOR?

Sitting there I felt more ridiculous and stupid by the second. Apparently, I was trying to prove to myself that I didn't make good business decisions, RIGHT??

More time passed. And what did I know about selling million-dollar listings? Or living in them, for that matter? NOTHING!

I was the kind of businessperson who rejects bigger deals because he's too afraid to handle them, because he's convinced he'll fail. Occasionally, someone would toss a great lead my way—one of my finance buddies who had a client with a $10 million budget looking for a place. Rather than seizing these huge opportunities I'd say, "Thanks, but that's not really my thing." *Whaaattt?* I was more comfortable clinging to the low-stakes, relatively hazard-free deals like rental leases with no tricky co-op board approvals. Those were just a basic credit check and, voilà, your keys! I was used to opting for the easy way to make a smaller dollar.

EVERYONE WILL LAUGH AT ME, my head screamed. This felt like the time back in Little League when I was so terrified in the outfield, my knees were shaking. I was completely clueless, and I was convinced that I was bad at baseball before I even tried. What do I do if the ball comes to me? Right—I try to catch it, *but then what do I do with it*?! What if I can't throw it far enough? Before I could have a full-on panic attack on the field, my father arrived. Right on the field, in front of everyone, he said, "Let's go, Ryan. Baseball isn't for you." I walked off the field with such shame, and yet I was relieved that I didn't have to try.

So much could go wrong at this audition. What if they ask me questions about elaborate real estate transactions and I don't know how to answer them? How did I ever think I could be on a TV show about real estate, a profession I had barely just started working in. My head ached. I COULD FAIL!

Wait, did they just call my name?

I extracted myself as quickly as I could from the depths of the ultra-plush velvet sofa. I walked quickly to the interview room while my eyes began searching for the winner. Someone in this hotel lobby was going to get on this show, and it obviously wasn't going to be me. Then I looked around the dimly lit lobby and realized it was impossible, even with that expensive lighting, to tell that I was any different from all the other brokers. I couldn't tell the top broker who was selling billions from guys like me. And then I thought, Wait, why not me? I have to be the guy who is killing it if I want this job. That's what they're looking for, and that's what I can give them.

I decided that while I might not be the best broker in Manhattan, the time to shine was now or never.

It felt scary, but I had to just go ahead and throw myself in. I didn't really feel like I could do it—but the Big version of Ryan could! Big Ryan was confident, put together, and knew his shit. I had thirty seconds to impress the casting people, so I was going to ramp up my energy and give them what they wanted—the best broker in the world.

After a basic introduction, we jumped right into the interview. The camera started rolling and the questions came at me fast: "So, Ryan, how do you get around the city?" Before I could whip out my unlimited-ride MetroCard, I said, "Black car by day, Range Rover by night."

Whoa, what? Who am I? I don't have a Range Rover, and I only had a black car that one time with June Shen! But I *could* have both if I needed to.

They hit me with the next question: "What is your favorite animal?" *What?* What kind of question—?! My mind started spinning for a good answer. *Don't say dog, everyone is going to say dog or lion or shark. Shark is obvious! Then what? Oh my God, I don't know. Go alphabetical!*

"Aardvark."

I thought I saw a hint of a smile pass over the casting director's face. Either they liked my unique answer or they thought I was a freak. "Aardvark? Really? Why?"

I shrugged casually like I had had dozens of conversations about aardvarks in my life. *Think, Serhant! What does an aardvark even look like?! Uhh . . .* "Well, because who needs ants, for one, and two, to survive in the concrete jungle of New York City you have to have a hard outer shell, just like an aardvark." Wow. I'm good. This is kind of fun! I was starting to relax, and I was ready for more jeopardy when they hit me with "How much do you sell?" *Well, shit.* I was ready to give a pithy answer about why magenta is my favorite color, but now . . . "Quite a lot. If you want the specific details it would take me a while to tell you, and I just don't have that kind of time today, I'm sorry."

Could they see the sweat starting to form on my big, white forehead?

"All right. We have one last question for you. Why should we pick you?" *Think, Ryan, what can you say to be memorable and not just another flippy-haired broker guy? What would Big Ryan say?*

"Because I'm the greatest fucking real estate broker in the history of the world." If I'd had a microphone, I would have dropped it (thankfully, I did not have one.)

CODE #2

If you need to mask your insecurities,
amplify the traits that are working for you.

And just like that, the interview was over. I left the audition feeling . . . *meh*. I just blew it. Why didn't I just tell them I was brand new and I'd be the perfect underdog for them? I didn't lie to them about anything. In the moment, I honestly believed I would one day be the best broker in the world—who could take that feeling away from me? But I could have just been honest and told them I was a loser who had only done a few deals and was self-conscious about his appearance too. And is it a known fact that psychopaths choose the aardvark as their favorite animal? Should I not have said that? I had no idea what to expect.

After several weeks of silence, I assumed it was over. Maybe the 300 brokers who were interviewed before me that day also announced that they were the "best in the world."

Just when I was about to push the audition out of my mind forever, an email arrived saying that I was still in the running (but don't get too excited, so were several hundred other brokers—they had initially interviewed over 3,000 of us).

Over the next few months, I did more Skype interviews with the casting director. They wanted to know what I was selling and what I would be willing to reveal on the show. "What's the biggest listing you have right now that we could film?" "Do you have a girlfriend or boyfriend, or both?" "Would you be nude on camera?" Well, I didn't have ANY big listings, I didn't have a girlfriend, and I didn't feel comfortable being naked in front of millions of people. So, I told them: "I have a $20 million–plus listing in SoHo coming up that would be good, I'm dating most of Manhattan right now, and when am I not naked, you know."

Perfect. They liked those answers. I was giving them the version of Ryan they wanted to put on TV—not the one who watched four hours of Saturday-morning cartoons and ate directly out of a cereal box. I gave them Ryan: amplified.

And I was also giving myself heart palpitations. A $20 million SoHo listing? How would I find THAT? Dating most of Manhattan? Who did I think I was—Mr. Sex and the City?? I had to make the projection of Big Ryan a reality. I started cold-calling past listings in SoHo that had come off the market. Not because I actually thought I could sell them (like a normal broker), but because I had put a meta-phorical SHOTGUN to my head by telling Bravo and NBC-Universal that I had a huge SoHo listing ready to film, and now they wanted proof.

I couldn't find anything, so I googled "SoHo penthouse," and an article in the *New York Post* came up about a guy who had this massive penthouse on Greene Street. Appar-ently, "Mr. Defendant" hadn't been paying his bills for a long, long, time and he was being sued by everyone in the building. That guy sounded like he needed to sell, and it turns out he was a pretty well-known photographer back in the day and his phone number was still up on his website. So, I called him.

"Hi, Mr. Defendant? This is Ryan Serhant, top broker in New York City. I am about to be cast on the biggest reality show to hit the universe, called *Million Dollar Listing New York*, and I'm looking for ONE mega-penthouse to film in. Interested?"

Silence.

"Hello?"

"Don't call me again." *Click.*

Small Ryan would have taken that for what it was and never called him again. But Big Ryan doesn't take no for an answer. And current Ryan NEEDS this listing to make Big Ryan happy. So, I called him again.

"Sorry—I don't think you heard me correctly. I can sell your apartment for around $20 million, help you pay off your debts, and we can do it on TV as a big FUCK YOU to everyone suing you. I'll even throw you a party with models and bottles. Let's meet. Is today at three or tomorrow at one better for you?"

"Three." *Click.*

I met Mr. Defendant that very same day. He looked tired and his dark, wavy hair was wild. I got the feeling that this guy might have been in a bar fight or two at some point during his life. He was a little scary, so I wanted to get right to the point: "I'm new to the industry, but I'm hungrier than a feral kitten and I won't rest until I sell your apartment." I must have said something right, because he gave me a tour. A long time ago he had combined four different apartments, creating a massive 10,000-square-foot palace for himself right in the middle of SoHo. The main living room had 30-foot ceilings and smack dab in the center of the room was a Harley Davidson motorcycle he had to have craned in. (He showed me the photo. He had to shut down Greene Street, causing major traffic headaches and infuriating everyone—but there was Mr. Defendant, smiling ear to ear. I think he got off on being bad.)

He let me list the apartment. I believe he did this out of pity for my feral kitten level of hunger, and because he was surprised I had the balls to cold-call him like that. I think he gave me about a .02% chance of actually selling it. He wanted to list at $25 million, which was an incredibly high asking price for his apartment. There was one contingency though: Mr. Defendant insisted on being on Bravo so he could show everyone suing him, including his "devil ex-wife," how cool he was. That is the story of how I got my first $25 million listing. I had an eight-figure SoHo penthouse ready to go contingent on it being on a TV show that I wasn't even cast on yet. Insert head-exploding emoji here.

THE THREE POINTS OF PERSUASION

1. Let it sink in: I wasn't surprised when Mr. Defendant hung up on me the first time I called. I needed to show some patience. I was a random stranger calling him up to ask if I could sell his apartment! I had to give him a moment to let the idea I had proposed start to sink in. When I called him back, the seed of the idea had already been planted, so when I opened with "I can get you millions of dollars for your apartment" I had his attention. If someone isn't completely open to your idea the first time around, give them a minute to absorb what you've proposed and then try again. Chances are you'll have better luck in round two.

2. Solve a problem: Mr. Defendant had a real problem: he was being sued and had tons of debt. Selling his apartment wouldn't be just a real estate transaction—it was a solution to his massive problems. Demonstrate how the idea you're proposing can make someone's life easier or eliminate a problem. *If we hire another team member, we can take on more projects, bring in more income—and bonus, the workload will be spread out and we won't have to work every single weekend!* It's hard for someone to say NO if they can clearly see the benefit to saying YES.

3. No room for NO: When you're trying to persuade someone to follow a proposed course of action, never ask a question they can say no to. People respond better if offered options. A yes-or-no decision easily leads to NO. "Do you want to buy this sweater?" is more likely to get you a negative response than "Did you want blue or green? They both looked great on you!" Practice phrasing your requests in a manner that leaves zero room to say NO.

The interviews pressed on. More Skypes and more written applications. Bravo is INTENSE. I presented evidence about deals I was working on, including my massive SoHo listing. The others were small but interesting—like the woman on the West Side who had a safe room for her designer clothes, and kept her closets padlocked so no one viewing her apartment could run off with a Chanel jacket. I was getting increasingly excited about this opportunity. I had always enjoyed acting, and being on a reality show would give me an opportunity to use my creative side while still working and paying my bills. And despite what my friends and family thought, being a real estate broker on a TV show would be like one giant commercial for my services. I figured the more people who knew I was a salesperson, the better. Imagine if one day I could walk down the street in New York and instead of no one noticing me, people would yell out their car window: "Hey! Aren't you that real estate guy from TV?!" As I got further along in the process, I saw the opportunity as a huge positive, and I wanted it to happen.

Finally, about six months after that initial interview when I blurted out that my favorite animal was an aardvark, a nocturnal insectivore sometimes known as the "earth pig," I got a call from the casting director.

"Hi, Ryan! We've narrowed it down to sixteen brokers and you're one of them. We are coming in from LA, and we'd like to have a film crew follow you for a few hours to see what a typical day is like for you. Just do whatever is normal. You know, don't think about it, don't plan anything."

Do what's normal? Normal for me was buying a bagel from the coffee cart on the street corner and eating it all before my client arrived, so they wouldn't see me with cream cheese on my face. Normal was hoping clients didn't notice I had giant armpit sweat stains from riding the hot subway. Normal was spending hours in front of a computer in an office that smelled like a hospital cafeteria.

I was working hard but it wasn't glamorous—I didn't have my own office or fancy lunches with clients like some brokers. Normal for me was not going to cut it.

I spent several nights pacing my empty apartment, thinking about how to present a picture of success to the casting crew. Then I made a decision. It wasn't going to be "my normal." There was no way I was going to leave it to chance that they'd be with me on a random Wednesday morning that wasn't busy. There was no guarantee I'd even have any showings for them to accompany me to. I spent a lot of my time doing follow-up or making cold calls while eating a sad desk salad in a room full of other brokers. That didn't exactly scream (a) success or (b) riveting television.

I had gotten so close to what I now saw was an amazing opportunity to grow my career that I was not going to let fate take control of my destiny. I wasn't going to let things happen to me. I was going to be deliberate and steer the course of my life. If I wanted to get this job, I had to show them what Big Ryan's day looked like. If they cast me and film me as the low-rent broker I am today, then people will see me that way all over the world when the show airs, and I'll only attract other low-rent clients, I thought. "Hey, dude, saw you on that show. Looks like things are tough and you're kind of down and out. Me too. So maybe you could help me find an apartment? My budget is $8.93." NO. I wanted great clients, with great BIG amounts of money, and those clients would only call me if they saw me as one of them: successful.

Once again, in order to succeed, I'd need to amplify.

Most days I would only get a handful of calls from clients looking for an apartment, or maybe a few calling to cancel appointments last minute. Other days I would be booked on the hour every hour, and it seemed like my phone never stopped ringing. THAT is the Ryan I wanted the casting directors to see.

And that's the Ryan I would give them. I needed to be booked left and right so I would appear to be super busy. I made several appointments, and I asked all of my friends and family to call me during the time I was with the casting people, just in case fate threw me a slower day. I wasn't going to leave how many calls I got to chance.

"Just call me between 7 A.M. and 12 P.M.," I told my friend Caleb, "and if I don't pick up, call again and keep calling until I answer!"

"Yeah, whatever, bro." *Click.*

I called this agent in our office named Mike who I did deals with sometimes. He had a Range Rover. "I need your car! I promise I will not wreck it." He sounded hesitant: "Wait, you don't have a dog do you? The last person I let borrow my car, her dog peed all over the back seat. It smelled like pee and wet dog hair for weeks."

"No dogs. I just need it to transport humans." I hoped it didn't still smell like pee and I hoped it wasn't hairy!

"Okay, just make sure you get it back by 5 P.M. because I'm driving out to Jersey to see my parents. And . . . Ryan . . . you've driven in the city before, right?"

"Thanks, Mike!" *Click.*

I told the casting crew to meet me at a boxing gym at 6 A.M. I hated boxing, so I will admit that the gym portion of the day I showed them was kind of bullshit. At the time, I thought you had to be a dick to be seen as a *boss*, but more on that later. I do work out every day, but with weights. But I wanted to look like a badass. And boxers are badasses, right? I wanted everyone in LA to watch my casting tape and say, "Hey, who is that badass boxing broker? So gritty! So New York! Cast him NOW!" Sounds good, right?

The day arrives. I'm at the gym throwing weird punches and awkwardly kicking a bag when the casting director, camera man, and audio guy came dragging in, obviously not pleased with it being the crack of dawn, given they were on West Coast time and jet-lagged. But they were still polite. I had told the main trainer, Eddie Lesinsky, who was this ultra-intense ex-army ranger, to just make me look good and tough. He said, "Say no more. I almost died fifteen times for this country. I know what to do." So, when the camera crew walked in, he started jumping up and down, yelling like a madman: "SERHANT, YOU READY TO GO? SERHANT, I CAN'T HEAR YOU?! SIR! HANT!?!" *What... is he doing?*

"Uh. YES! YES! LET'S GOOOO!"

"Let me hear you ROARRRRRR!" The casting crew was staring at us as if they were watching a UFC cage match. I couldn't tell what level of terrified they were. But they started filming. Eddie jumped in the ring with me and started fighting ME. "Eddie ... Eddie ..." I said, totally out of breath. "Dude, you're at a level 199 right now, bring it down to an 8 and just box with me. I don't want to die."

"Ah. You got it, bro." We started sparring but he kept yelling regardless.

Next they wanted to see where a top New York City broker lived. While I was making more money than when I first started out, I didn't have a pile of spare cash sitting around to decorate what was actually a nice apartment in the financial district. Nothing screams new-college-graduate-with-entry-level-job quite like an empty apartment. A week before the shoot I went to the furniture department at Macy's. I walked through the sample living rooms and bedrooms, looking for the ones that suggested good taste and class. "I'll take those two rooms please!" I handed over my credit card and bought two entire rooms of furniture, thinking that I would probably be paying for this stuff forever. What's the fun in having a high-interest-rate credit card if you don't get to pay it off forever?

We all piled into the Range Rover, the film crew in the back seat. I took a big breath before pulling out into the street. I was careful not to show it, but I was terrified. I had never, ever, not once been behind the wheel of a car in New York City. Let alone someone else's $90,000 car. Driving in Manhattan is like being dropped into a real-life video game—you have to dodge speeding taxis, buses, trucks, countless food delivery bikes, and clueless humans who are glued to their phones and can step in front of your car at any time. When my friend bravely handed over the keys to his car, he provided a warning: "People get into accidents in the city because they are being overly safe." Fuck it. Big Ryan doesn't play it safe. I floored it. The crew freaked out. They were hanging on to the side of the car while filming me driving like a maniac. As we flew downtown at breakneck speed I shouted into the back seat about points of interest: "If you look to your left, you'll see the famous Wall Street bull!" And hey, "Did you guys see Trinity Church and Alexander Hamilton's tombstone? Yeah, well we just passed that. You know, to be the best in New York you have to play offense 24/7, even while driving! HAHAHA." I swear, I think the sound guy peed himself just a little bit (sorry, Mike!).

Miraculously, and much to the relief of the now nauseous crew, we made it to my apartment in one piece. Just as I had hoped, my phone was ringing like crazy, "The Saudi's wire didn't go through? Okay. No worries, I'll get back to you." The crew was looking around my apartment, noticing my surfboard (my friend's), road bike (other friend's), and long board (first friend's) as I got dressed. I kept taking calls as I was straightening my tie. "Hi. Yeah, that's great that they want to make an offer—$3.4 million? I'm not sure that's going to be enough, unless you want to split the difference with me. I can afford it, but not sure about you. I'll call you back."

I took another call in the elevator. "Hi, Ryan, it's your mother. You told me to call you. What's going on? Why are you in such a hurry?" I responded, "Yes. I'm thrilled you want to put your place on the market. I'll have my assistant send over the paperwork."

"Your what? You don't have an assistant, Ryan. This is your MOTHER! What are you talking about? Are you okay?"

My phone kept ringing as the crew reluctantly got back into my death car, so I could drive us to Gramercy where I was showing a three-bedroom penthouse to a banker. When I met my client (who was legit, NOT a friend, and who miraculously agreed to let a film crew capture the showing as long as it never aired anywhere) it was clear he was having a bad day. He had a crumpled *Wall Street Journal* under one arm and a half-eaten bacon-egg-and-cheese bagel sandwich in his other hand. "The market sucks today, so I hope you're not wasting my time with this apartment."

The crew watched anxiously as I showed the angry banker the great view he'd have from his master bedroom. By the time I showed him the rest of the apartment—the chef's kitchen with the granite island, the top-of-the-line appliances, and 12-foot ceilings with floor-to-ceiling windows overlooking the city—his mood had notably improved. He was interested in the apartment . . . yes!

When my client left, I took a quick glance at the time. *Fuck*. It was only 10 A.M. How is that possible? I felt as if my stomach had suddenly dropped from the penthouse directly down to the basement. I was supposed to let them follow me around for three more hours. Ugh! This was all supposed to take much longer! I literally had nothing else to do. No showings. No meetings. The one other showing I was going to take them to bailed on me while we were speeding through the city. The film crew stood there waiting to see what was next. How was I going to deal with this? Top brokers do not have slow moments! You don't make millions by doing nothing.

FLIP THE SCRIPT

As I was thinking about how I was going to improvise three more hours of acting like I was a big-time broker, my phone rang. "Hi, my name is Mary and I'm calling about the one-bedroom you have listed for rent for $1,900 per month in Chelsea? Can I see it?"

I couldn't take the film crew to this listing, since it was most definitely not a million-dollar listing.

While Mary continued to talk about what she was looking for, and asking if the apartment was dog friendly and if it was okay that her dad would be paying the rent for her, I went into the bathroom. Sweating about my fate while listening to Mary's Long Island accent, I suddenly remembered a date I had gone on not too long ago.

I had met a girl for drinks and we were headed to get dinner next, but then her phone rang just as we were walking out of the bar. After she hung up, she looked at me and said, "Ryan, I am having such a good time with you. Really, this is great! I'm so sorry though, I have to leave. I'll call you later." She was super nice about it while not being overly apologetic. She tossed just the littlest dash of "I don't care" my way before she confidently walked out the door. I wasn't upset at all. She just seemed confident, strong, and in control . . . all while being nice. I was like, Wow. I definitely want to go out with her again. She just rejected me with class on the go.

"Hello? Are you even there? Can you show me the apartment?" I focused my attention back on Mary. I quickly gave her the address and told her I'd meet her in twenty minutes. I hung up the phone and went back out to the film crew. "I am so incredibly sorry. Something big has just come up and I must deal with it immediately. Really, if you need anything more from me at all, just call." I gave them three phone numbers "in case they couldn't get me on the first one," but they would definitely get me on the first one because the other numbers weren't real. Only my mom called me every day, but when people think you are so busy that you need three phones, it automatically changes their perception of you. "Again, I apologize but it can't be helped. I'll get you whatever you need." And with that kind, but clear dash of "I don't care," I left them alone in the apartment and I checked out with class, looking confident, strong, and in control. I could see them watching me out the window from the penthouse as I got into my friend's Range Rover and forgot how to start it. Ah . . . push to start. And I was off. *Holy. Shit.*

It would be several more *looonnng* months before I learned that I would be cast on the premiere season of

EMERGENCY EXIT POWER LINES

Sometimes we find ourselves at work in situations that we need to get out of—immediately. Whether it's a meeting that's running too long, a phone call you just can't get off of, or a client who doesn't get the hint that you have to get to another appointment (or you're trying to save your face like pre-BME Ryan with the film crew), use one of these lines to end the conversation and extract yourself from the situation gracefully.

- "Something suddenly came up that I have to handle right away. I'm so sorry!"

- "I'm so glad we got to start this process, I look forward to the next steps and I'll get back to you ASAP."

- "You know what? I think we've established our objective! I'll be in touch about how to continue. Thanks!"

- "I wish I didn't have the rest of my morning booked so we could continue this conversation. This has been great, but my next appointment is on the way."

- "I'm so glad I got to meet you. I'll touch base with you about this tomorrow."

Million Dollar Listing New York, to one day air to 25 million people around the world. While I don't think ditching the film crew was the moment that made the casting director think, "Yes! We want him!" I do believe that things would have ended differently if I hadn't flipped the script back in my favor. Cutting the day short wasn't ultimately about controlling the situation; it was about properly managing a positive perception of myself. I needed to maintain the perception that I was *busy-busy-busy* making huge deals all day long. I was often busy during that time. I was making more big deals—but I had to manage the perception in that specific moment, or it would look like I wasn't doing much of anything at all, and no one cares about what your life is like when they're not watching. Back when I was trying to be a model, I remember there were days where I'd have an audition and on that day, of all days, I'd get a big zit right in the middle of my forehead. Why couldn't the audition have been on a clear-skin day? Now the casting director is going to think I have zits on my forehead ALL the time and won't cast me, I'd think. And that's exactly what would happen. I wasn't going to let that happen to me now, or ever again. If I hadn't flipped the script, the crew would have watched me eat lunch at my desk, return phone calls, and write a bunch of emails . . . *not thrilling stuff*. That's not BIG. They would have listened to me tell stories about busy days I'd had previously, and about crazy phone calls from the week before. And they would have been bored. People with Big Money Energy understand that there is no magic moment when you leave small energy behind forever to transform permanently into something bigger and more powerful. There will always be moments when life throws you something unexpected, when the perception of who you are can be challenged. A core part of having BME is holding on to the perception that you're strong, confident, and in control, even when it feels like you aren't.

As I continued driving downtown (more slowly this time) to my rental client, I realized that while, yes, I might have

---

CODE #3

Fill your mind with positive thoughts for at least
ten seconds before meeting anyone. If your head
is in a good place, you'll exude positivity and
confidence, and it will set the tone for the meeting.

---

ditched the film crew and I might never get on this show,
I had proven to myself that I was capable of taking concrete steps to control my energy. I had learned that it was
Big Ryan who embodied what I wanted in life. It was Big
Ryan who drove that Range Rover, who got up early to box
with an army ranger, who juggled phone calls easily, had a
great showing, and most importantly—was able to hold it
all together the very moment it all could have fallen apart.
Saying, "Well. Sorry guys. I know it's only 10 A.M. but that's
all I've got going on, want to get pancakes?" was not going
to help my transformation into Big Ryan. I controlled the
narrative; I didn't let the reality of the situation control me.
I understood that day that I had the power to take back control of my life just by changing my energy.

I parked the Range Rover, and my phone rang as I was
walking over to the building on West 8th Street to meet
Mary and her dad. It was the banker who had seen the
penthouse this morning—he thought the camera crew was
kind of cool, and he wanted to make an offer.

CHAPTER 3

AMATEUR HOUR IS OVER

To: ryan@ryanserhant.com

From: Big Time Casting Director

Hi Ryan:

I'm a big fan of MDLNY! I'm casting a new movie with Ben Stiller, Naomi Watts, Adam Driver and Amanda Seyfried, directed by Noah Baumbach, and I was wondering if you wanted to audition for the role of "Hedge Fund Dave"? I think you'd be great in the role.

Let me know,

Doug

It had been four years since I had kissed my acting career goodbye and settled into my role as a broker, so I deleted that email right after I read it. Acting was dead to me! Sure, I'd like to audition for your "movie." I'd also like to have the power of invisibility! And you know what else would be great? If I could fly! I had spent years of my life trying to get in front of big-name directors like Noah Baumbach AND FAILING. The email had to be a joke. I pushed it out of my mind and got back to work.

A couple of weeks later, I came across another message when I was doing my 4:45 A.M. pre-gym email check.

To: ryan@ryanserhant.com

From: Big Time Casting Director

   Hi Ryan: Just wondering if you've thought about the audition? I think you'd be great as Hedge Fund Dave. Let me know if you have any questions. I've attached the pages from the script that feature the character you'd be auditioning for.

Wait. Maybe this was real? Would anyone actually write a script as part of a joke? That would be taking things really far. I quickly skimmed through the pages. It was good too! And funny! Apparently Hedge Fund Dave takes a meeting with Josh (Ben Stiller's character) to hear his pitch about why he should invest in the world's longest and most boring documentary. Hedge Fund Dave's lines were dry and sarcastic—he was just like me. But too bad, because I had given up acting FOREVER! Apparently hope springs eternal, because there was a little voice in my head that would not *shut up*: "You know you want to audition, Ryan. A real director approaches and you think you can just walk away? It's not like last time—you can easily afford groceries now. You won't starve to death if you don't land the role!" The annoying voice in my head was right. I had to give this a shot. I responded to the email saying I'd love to be considered. What a cool opportunity!

   The day of the audition I headed to the address in the East Village I'd been given. When I opened the door, it was like I was having a bad flashback. I had walked right into a scene from my failed acting career: wall-to-wall actors, mostly dressed in jeans and T-shirts, all desperate to land a role. Everyone was reading scripts, some were pacing back and forth reciting their lines, a couple of guys were fake-sparring, and one was staring at the wall while he repeated the warm-up "Unique New York, Unique New York" over and over again. These people are intense! I swear the walls were actually pulsing with all of this nervous energy. It's an audition; it's not like we have to improvise open heart surgery! It was a relief to see that for once, I wasn't the only nervous guy doing the small face–big face warm-up I learned in acting school, which always makes me look crazy. This time I was the guy in the suit who had an open house later that afternoon that I had to prepare for because *I had a real job now, bitches.*

I stepped over a guy who was meditating in the lotus position on the floor and sat down in an empty chair. The ultra-jumpy wannabe actors could do their thing, but I needed to check my emails. A solid offer on that two-bedroom in Chelsea had come in. I bet I can get the buyer to raise her offer! I returned the email asking for a counter and had just finished answering the rest of my emails when I heard "Ryan Serhant! We are ready for you!"

As I walked out of the waiting area, I quickly glanced at the time—*Fuck.* I had been waiting so long that my open house uptown was starting in just twenty minutes! I needed to get in and out of here quickly. Now I was just annoyed I had even agreed to this stupid audition that wouldn't lead to anything anyway. I was led into a small room for the audition. The casting director explained she would be reading Ben Stiller's lines. Okay great, let's do this, I thought.

We launch into the scene, I'm doing my lines, and it's going well! I'm glad to hear a few laughs from the producers who are sitting in the room. Wow! *This is fun! I've never actually enjoyed an audition before.* Usually I was worried everyone could see my heart pounding through my shirt!

We finished the scene and the casting director thanked me for my time. I hustled myself past all of the hungry-looking actors (literally hungry; someone should feed these guys) and practically threw myself in front of the first available taxi I saw. On the ride uptown I checked my messages, and *yes* . . . I made it to my open house on time (a Manhattan traffic miracle!). It was a win-win kind of day.

The next day, I got an unexpected call at the office from the casting director: "Hi, that was the best audition we saw all day. We want you to audition with Ben." *Whoa. Ben . . . Stiller? For real?* The one time I don't care about getting a role, the one time I'm not practically chewing on the furniture waiting to see if I get a callback—this is the one time that it works?

A few days later, I was scheduled to meet with Ben Stiller and Noah Baumbach at a studio on 36th Street. The space was almost like a WeWork for actors: there are studios rented out for auditions and rehearsals. I get up to the designated floor and I realize, Wait a minute . . . I think I've been here before. Yes! This is the exact same place where we had weekly story meetings with the producers for *MDLNY* during season one! For a quick second I'm reminded of how far I've come since the show started. *MDLNY* was like the proverbial gun to the head. I went from hanging on by my teeth, hoping the producers wouldn't kick me off, and now I'm here to do a scene with Ben Stiller! What a crazy coincidence!

At that moment one of the assistants calls me into the room. I walk in, and sitting right in front of me is Noah

Baumbach, director, and *Zoolander himself.* I freeze. Everyone is staring at me and then I just blurt out: "Hi. I've been in this room before." Both of them just look at me. Then Noah says, "Oh."

I couldn't get over the fact that I was about to meet BEN FUCKING STILLER in the real estate reality TV producers' office?! What is life, honestly? But this time I'm not just a wretched wannabe actor who would give two kidneys to get an audition like this. I was *invited* to be here. And when I'm done, I'm going to walk out of this room and head downtown to pick up a six-figure commission check. I felt energized.

Ben says, "Are you ready to do this?" *Yeah, I am.* And I play it like I already have the role. We're doing the scene and then Ben Stiller actually starts laughing! I made Zoolander laugh! We even had to do the scene over because of it—it was great.

The next day, I am standing in a $20 million penthouse apartment on Eleventh Avenue with its own car elevator when I get a call from Doug, the casting director. "Ryan, we want to offer you the role." After all those failed attempts, I was going to get to see my name on a movie screen. All I had to do was give up on acting and get into real estate. Holy shit!

GET OVER YOURSELF

It's not like I magically became a better actor the day I auditioned with Ben, but I had become a different person since my last foray into the acting world. I used to be just like those other actors,* frantically studying lines, hands shaking from nerves—I'd basically walk into auditions with my guts laid out before me. *Hire me! Please pick me! Over here . . . me me me me me!* My nervous energy easily overshadowed any talent I had to offer. I was a little puppy nipping at people's heels for attention.† And people don't want to do business or work with (or make movies) with puppies. Puppies jump up and down pleading for treats. Puppies beg for someone to just toss them a stupid ball. Puppies are small and can't manage their frantic energy. Puppies . . . *will pee on your stuff.* Now, for contrast, let's turn the conversation to the magnificent lupus, otherwise known as *the wolf.* Wolves have *control* . . . Wolves don't need to be petted to know they're awesome. And you certainly don't tell a wolf to "go fetch." Wolves don't fuck around. If a wolf is hungry, he just sniffs the air, zooms in on his prey, and *goes and gets what he wants.*

Old Ryan would go into auditions with the weight of the world on his shoulders—bills, rent, no future, groceries. I had no focus! That is what *amateurs do.* Did the people who landed the roles I wanted have fears about bills and money? Maybe? Probably! Some of them must have, but they knew how to put their fears aside and come off like total pros. They only have $13 left in their bank account? Doesn't matter! That problem isn't going to cloud their audition. Pros can rise above—pros know that if they want something

---

*Some of those actors were probably amazing. For the sake of this story I'm focusing on the ones that were nervous wrecks.

†I know puppies are cute. I'm making a business analogy, so please just go with it.

badly enough, they need to be wolves sniffing out their next BIG kill. And guess what? Their bank balance will still have that shitty $13 after they slay that day . . . or not.

CODE #4

Don't be afraid to fail.
Your life's worth isn't determined
by a single moment.

I certainly didn't wake up one morning and see a great, big, ferocious wolf staring back at me in the mirror. This wasn't an overnight transformation! Early in my career it was *amateur hour all of the time*. Every job was life or death. Every rejection pummeled my self-worth. *Show me you love me! Would someone just throw me a ball!* But somewhere during my journey I managed to shed my amateur behaviors like a dirty jacket. Along the way, I discovered that at different points in my life, a few common insecurities were holding me back. They ate up my positive energy and made me feel small and incapable. If you want to speed up your transformation from amateur to pro, if you want to be bigger, you need to eliminate the following amateurish behaviors from your life immediately.

Stop Playing the Blame Game

This is a very, very dangerous game. I should know because I played it for years. The rules of this game are simple: The problem is never you. Someone or something is always at fault! There is a concrete reason, totally out of your control, for every problem, loss, and disappointment in your life. Sound familiar? It could be your circumstances. It could be what you don't have (money, connections, time, looks). It could be a boss or colleague who is hating on you. And if Mercury is in retrograde (when isn't it?) you can score ten bonus blame points!

Common phrases uttered during the blame game include "I would if," "except that," "but, if only," and "someday." If you are into playing this game, ask yourself—seriously, what are you getting out of it? You must hold yourself accountable for where you are in life. It's certainly easier for everything that's wrong with your life to be someone else's fault, because that means you don't have any work to do! But spoiler alert: NO ONE EVER WINS THIS STUPID GAME. Throw it out and be accountable for your actions, because you deserve to live out your awesome potential!

The next time things don't go your way, be brutally honest with yourself. Force yourself to write down three things you could have done to get a different outcome. The next time you give that group presentation, record yourself first. This way you're more prepared. Are you coming off as powerful and confident? Are you speaking clearly? Watching yourself will help you get the results you want. Blaming Tammy for farting loudly during your presentation won't. Practice until you come off like the pro you are. In the end, it's always the amateurs who sit on the sidelines while the pros get to play.

Manage Your Work PTSD

Just a few months ago my wife, Emilia, and I were able to take a long, solo weekend away on a tropical island. If you have kids, you know what a huge gift it is to be able to turn your baby over to a loving grandparent and get away (we are eternally grateful, Yiayia)! When I was lying on the beach I thought, This is so pretty! I should post a picture on Instagram! After posting the picture I lay back down, enjoying the warmth of the Caribbean sun on my face. I was wondering if I had applied an adequate amount of sunscreen when I heard the *ping!* of a text message. I took a peek and saw that it was from a developer I work with.

"Hi. I see that you're away this weekend."

I felt the blood drain from my face. *Oh my God, Ryan, you've really done it now. What were you thinking posting that picture? You're going to get fired—while on vacation! Way to go, BUDDY!*

Okay, wait. So, maybe tell him the picture is from last year? But that's a lie—and you're not a liar!

I sat up and looked around at the beautiful beach. So, what if I am on vacation! I needed to get a grip. I am a grown man, I thought, in charge of my own life. I have a great team who is hard at work back in the city taking care of this client's listings. I shouldn't be afraid of him thinking, "Oh, look! Ryan's gallivanting around an island. Clearly, he doesn't care about me or my apartments. Ryan sucks! He's fired!" I genuinely, truly believed my business could fall apart if I admitted that I occasionally took time away from work to relax. No listings were being hurt while I sat here baking on the beach. Of course I could take a weekend off! I wrote back:

"Yep. Away with my wife this weekend! We're having a great time, hope you're well!"

I swallowed hard when I hit "send." I immediately saw text bubbles. Text bubbles! I was being taunted by text bubbles. Just as I was about to get up and throw myself into the ocean, he responded:

"Looks really cool! You totally deserve it!"

I might have made it to the number-one slot several years in a row—I was literally the number-one broker in the WORLD! But I think most of us still have work PTSD, when our worst moments haunt us.

The time when someone said something so small, but so deeply terrible that it's been with you for fifteen years. "You're not good enough" meant "you're not worthy." That moment comes back to you so often that you feel a constant need to overcompensate for it, hence murdering that person's remark over and over again. It's easier to remember those gut-wrenching moments than it is to recall the countless days at work that went . . . *just fine*. Or the tons and bucketloads of compliments you've received for your work. After that brief but harrowing moment on the beach, I vowed to identify these PTSD moments as they appear so I can squash them before they take over. When that horrible sense of work-related panic hits you, ask yourself—is this real? Own it, correct it, and move on. Or, is this *NOT REAL*? You could be freaking out because this has the all-too-familiar feel of something shitty that went down in your past work experience.

A few years ago I had gotten fired from a job on the day of my wedding—and I was on an island! Doesn't that suck? It's no wonder that I freaked out on the beach. When I read the text from the developer that simply said, "I see that you're away this weekend," I initially read it as something like:

"Why are you so terrible at your job? I can't believe I ever trusted you, you lazy wannabe piece of trash, and I hope you get stung repeatedly by a swarm of giant jellyfish."

Going forward, I had to learn to deal with my PTSD by asking myself, "Am I reading attitude into this that doesn't actually exist?" Just because I interpreted the text to be a jab at my work ethic doesn't mean it was. I was having a work PTSD hot flash. Train yourself on how to handle your PTSD. You need to determine if you are letting something from your past infect your present. Some of you are walking around with some deep-rooted PTSD issues on a daily basis. Some of your staff may be on the receiving end of that. Identify your triggers.

I had to understand first that even if I didn't have a team to handle my client's listings that weekend, I would have still deserved a weekend off. No one owns my time but me. I also have to tell myself on a daily basis that there will always be some people who CANNOT BE PLEASED. Work 24/7, go above and beyond, consistently deliver fantastic results, offer your firstborn child—and they're still unhappy. If your PTSD is tied to human reactions that have upended your livelihood, the solution here is to simply say (in your mind, please) "FTG!"

"FTG" means Fuck That Guy! If you're having a PTSD moment, FTG can be a very eloquent, resolving solution. You have to let it go, and quickly. You have to learn to let any negativity roll right off your back. If it's a situation that drives you crazy, it's "FTS": Fuck That Situation. FTG or FTS are instant healing mechanisms. Try them at your own risk.

IDENTIFY WORKPLACE TRIGGERS

Workplace triggers come in many forms and they are The Worst. Triggers can make your palms sweat, your stomach turn, your throat dry—and worst of all, they can make you doubt your own ability. Learn what your workplace triggers are, so you can identify and slay these beasts every time they rear their ugly heads. The following is a general list of awful things that some of us have experienced that leave us wanting to fight or flee. If any of these are familiar to you, do the work to banish these memories from your psyche!

- Getting fired.
- Overlooked for a promotion.
- A co-worker got the promotion you wanted.
- Shot down or criticized at a meeting for an idea no one liked.
- Horrible boss.
- Missed a deadline and the project tanked.
- Watched your boss take credit for all your hard work.
- Got left off an email chain about a new project.
- Crazy and impossible clients.
- Weren't invited to the after-work cocktails with your co-workers.
- The terrible typo that made you look stupid—"public" and "pubic," they're so close!
- That time you "replied all" on an email that "no way would I go to the staff holiday party because most of the people I work with are soooooo boring."

Flaws Can't Hold You Hostage

I suffered from a skin disorder well into my twenties that obliterated my self-confidence. I had always been acne prone, which was bad enough, but my face was also fire-engine red from rosacea, a skin condition that affects older women in the Midwest, and me. My face felt and looked like it was on fire. In college I slept with a special ice-pack mask to cool down my inflamed face. When I was an actor, I used to fret about it constantly—what roles suited a pimply fire-engine face? Elderly burn victim? Phantom of the Opera? The skin issues were crushing to my confidence, and I made the decision to do whatever it took to fix it. I found a dermatologist who suffered from the same condition, and I contacted him. His name is Dr. Nase, if you're wondering. I followed his advice. I removed all triggers like caffeine and sugar and apples, oddly enough, and I took low-dose Accutane for years. I worked construction jobs to earn money for expensive VBeam laser treatments that shrink the size of the blood vessels in your face while also peeling off your skin to bring out your inner Freddy Kreuger for a short period of time. Until I solved this problem, I could not look people in the eye. I stared at the ground when talking to people because I was so self-conscious about my red zits. It involved a lot of trial and error, but eventually I found the right balance of treatments and I had completely NORMAL, clear skin. That's all I wanted. And I am grateful I made the decision to change my skin every single day. Controlling my weight when I was younger, and then my skin, both saved my life and taught me that I had willpower beyond what I initially thought possible.

I'm not saying you need to have flawless skin to succeed in life. That's not true! But if something is crushing your spirit so hard that you really believe it's keeping you from realizing your full wolf potential, consider making a change. You owe it to yourself to walk out the door with your head held up proudly every single day.

But then there are the flaws we *can* learn to live with, the flaws that are actually *character*.

If you said to a friend right now, "Hey, I'm reading this great new book by that guy Ryan from *Million Dollar Listing New York*!" they'd likely say, "Wait. Which one is he again?"

I would bet my left pinky finger that you would say, "The funny one with the gray hair." And they'd say, *"Ohhhh,* right. That guy."

If younger Ryan who went gray at sixteen knew that his cursed gray hair would become his calling card, he could have saved A LOT of time and money dying his hair. My hair makes me stand out because, let's face it, most people my age are not completely gray. Character is that part of you that's different, interesting, eye catching, and maybe even alluring or sexy . . . even if it doesn't feel that way to you (yet!).

Life is hard enough, but I believe that we often make it harder on *ourselves* (I know I did). For years I was walking around burdened by my skin, my hair, my weight, my rent, my anxiety, and my fear of failure. They were like heavy dumbbells I carried with me all day long—to auditions, to job interviews, to parties, even to the negotiating table some years into my career. Carrying all of that baggage was exhausting. I was depressed and worn out. I had to put the past in the past. Those days are behind me. It's time to set that weight down . . . Wow, that felt good! The burden we all carry around can be so heavy! Shake it off. Get over yourself. Then see what happens when you're lighter, freer, and ready to grab life by the throat.

YOUR FLAWS ARE DEAD TO YOU

When I played the super-awesome but eventually very dead Dr. Evan Walsh IV on the soap opera *As the World Turns*, I got exactly one note from the executive producer. I was excited to get feedback on my acting. I walked into the office and the executive producer looked up at me and said, "Why is your skin so pale and your hair so dark? You look like a fucking vampire. Okay, you can go back to set." *What?* It took years of dying my hair and spending tons of money to even get close to creating an undead look! As you can see from my book cover, it never happened all the way. I had to make a choice to embrace the gray. It took me ages to stop seeing my hair as a flaw and embrace it as character. The bottom line was that no one ever really cared that I had gray hair (that was all me). We all have flaws, and the truth is life gets a lot easier when you accept them and devote your energy towards living a bigger and better life. So, make a pact with yourself right now. (No, put down your phone. I mean now, dammit!) Commit to yourself: "I will accept my flaws." If you're the shortest guy in the office, who cares? You know who else is short (allegedly)? *Tom Cruise.* In order to establish a real pact, you must agree to the following:

I, _Daniel James_ (YOUR NAME HERE), vow to accept and embrace _my height_ (YOUR FLAW HERE). I promise from this day forward not to complain about it, blame it for holding me back in any aspect of my life, or spend valuable time obsessing over it. From now on I see _my height_ (YOUR FLAW) for what it really is: an important part of my character that I'll never speak ill of again!

Sign your name _____

Date __4/18/22__

BIG MONEY ENERGY

MANTRA #1

You can't commit to GOING BIGGER if there's even a small part of you that just doesn't believe it's possible. This mantra will help you shed any doubt (no matter how microscopic it might be!) that you are capable of achieving success on the highest levels. YOU have what it takes.

I AM FIERCE

I AM BOLD

I HAVE CONTROL

I HAVE BIG MONEY ENERGY

THE BLUEPRINT: GO BIGGER

You've committed to the idea that you want to live a bigger and better life, and I WANT THIS FOR YOU TOO! Remember that you have the power to do this, okay? YOU are in control NOW. We all started out in control, but somewhere along the way that control was stolen, stomped on, and crushed up in a ball and thrown in the trash. The first step to living a bigger life is taking back that control, and that starts with knowing who you want to be.

Imagine the picture of success you want to present to the world—go BIG. Does the picture of your life look like what you *really, really* want?

STEP ONE: Get Over Yourself
 - Stop playing the blame game.
 - Manage your work PTSD.
 - Don't let your flaws hold you hostage.

STEP TWO: Flip the Script
 - **If things aren't going in the direction you'd like them to go, take control.** You have the power to alter the outcome of a situation.
 - **Do not leave things up to chance.** Take concrete steps to show people the bigger, future you TODAY.
 - **Master the power of perception.** Life will throw you crazy challenges and you have to hold on to the perception that you're strong, confident, and in control.

STEP THREE: Master the Three Points of Persuasion
Use this tool to get people to do what you want.

- **Let it sink in.** Give the person time to absorb what you're saying.
- **Solve a problem.** Present someone with a solution to a problem to get their attention.
- **There is no room for no.** Avoid yes-or-no questions. Give choices instead.

STEP FOUR: Be a Wolf, Not a Puppy
The world wants to work with pros, not amateurs.

BUILD UP YOUR BME
An Exercise

When I was an actor, I'd prepare for roles by creating believable characters. I'd think about everything, from what they looked like and what kind of clothes they wore, to how their homes were decorated and how they walked and talked. You can use these same ideas to visualize a bigger life for yourself and recast the role that you are playing. I had to fire low-rent Ryan and replace him with a bigger, more commanding version of myself. This is your life we are talking about, so you have to THINK HUGE. You need to have a big vision for how you want other people to see you. To start to think of yourself in a bigger way, imagine seeing that version of yourself walking into a room. What do you look like? How do you walk? How do people respond to your presence? Spend some time describing what you see when YOU walk in! Can you see it? Great. Now, tomorrow morning when you wake up, don't think about being that person—BE THAT PERSON. What is that person like? Write it out.

That person is confident in his abilities. He knows his shit, and everyone else knows it too. He has white boy swagger oozing from his pores. He is the baddest motherfucker you've ever dealt with.

DIRECT YOUR LIFE
An Exercise

I would not be where I am today if I left that meeting with the *MDLNY* casting people 100% up to chance. They would have ended up seeing low-rent Ryan, and I can't think of anyone who would want to watch that guy on TV (other than maybe my mother). I stepped away from that day understanding that I DO have the power to shape the course of my day. It's up to me from the moment I wake up to chart the course of action towards greater success. I can go to the gym and get stronger, or I can sit back with a gigantic plate of waffles and put myself in a carb coma. You are the director of your own life. Do you want your movie to feature a sad, depressed guy who has dreams of leaving his accounting job to start his own company, and decades later he's sitting in the same office thinking, I SHOULD HAVE STARTED MY OWN COMPANY!? I never want to feel that kind of regret, and I never want you to feel that either. If you're saying, "If only I could move/quit/switch careers/go back to school/start my own business," what's keeping you from taking steps to do it? Think about it—what do you want? And how can you push yourself to take that first step? Write it out.

I want to have so much money that I can't figure out what to do with it all. I want to be important. I want to be handsome and adored.

MONEY

Money might not be everything, but you know it plays a major role in your life. Being alive can be expensive. On the most basic level, money represents survival and freedom, but you don't want to live a basic life. You work hard and crave a great life and all the accoutrements that come along with it. For you, more money means that you get to be free to live your life however you want.

CHAPTER 4

PEOPLE WHO EARN MORE

Right after I closed that seven-figure deal with June Shen I thought I was *the shit*. So, I convinced my friend Matt who works in commercial real estate to get me a meeting with a big-time real estate developer named Gordon Murray, who owned buildings all over Manhattan and South America. Even though I had only made one big sale, I honestly believed I could be a huge asset to him. "Surely, I can handle a 200-unit sell-out on the Upper West Side, Gordy boy!"

As I was riding the subway uptown, packed in with the rush hour crowd, I imagined that I could soon kiss the subway goodbye forever. When I arrived at Gordon's office in Times Square, I sat in an expensive-looking chair, buzzing with excitement about all the great opportunities this meeting could bring. When Gordon's assistant told me he was ready for me, I took a deep breath and said to myself, *You are awesome*.

When I entered Gordon's office, I shook his hand and he gestured to a chair across from him. He was tapping his pen on a legal pad. "So, Ryan, what do you think about the plans for Hudson Yards? Think Related will be able to pull it off given the current state of the retail market?"

I felt my complexion start to shift from white to bright pink. *Shit. I have no idea what you are talking about*, I thought. "It sounds really cool and I think they'll do great," I said.

Gordon pushed his legal pad and pen to the side. "How about HFZ's planned conversion of 344 West 72nd? And what do you think about the rezoning challenges in Hudson Square and Gowanus—what are your thoughts on how the lobbyists' efforts will affect the resi landscape in the next five to ten?" Fuckity Fuckerstein. I still didn't know what he was talking about, so I launched into a super-enthusiastic, passionate speech all about my one big sale to June Shen. I didn't stop to think about how I didn't really answer any of his questions, or that being unprepared would now mean that I'd have nothing to really talk about, which led me to go on and on about myself. Thinking back on this meeting makes me want to throw up. Gordon looked at his watch. "Okay, I have another meeting in a second. Thanks for coming in, kid."

Despite my total lack of preparation and Gordon's obvious disinterest in an arrogant "kid" who had made one deal, I somehow left that meeting thinking I had nailed it. I don't know why, but as I walked back to my office I had visions of depositing even bigger checks due to my new-found awesome connection with mega-developer Gordon Murray—$50,000 checks? Shit, $75,000, $100,000 . . . That's huge!

A few days later, I connected with my friend Matt who had gotten me the meeting. "Like, tell me what he said about me, man," I said. I was anxious to hear what Gordon thought. But then there was an awkward silence before Matt spoke: "Sorry, man. He said you seemed like a nice kid, but you have a long way to go." *What?????*

Is it possible it didn't go as well as I thought it did?!* I had walked into Gordon Murray's office thinking I was the best real estate broker in the universe . . . and to hear that I didn't come off well was soul crushing. And "a long way to go"? Oh my God, I couldn't imagine spending the next five, ten years renting and selling cheap apartments. How could I land those bigger projects and make millions if I came off as amateurish? The meeting only lasted fifteen minutes or so—and in that short of a time he assessed that I had no idea what I was doing. I felt like such a JERK.

In the brutal lens that retrospect provides, I can see that I was all swagger and no substance, and those qualities were not going to get me access to higher-paying jobs.

I walked into Gordon Murray's office unprepared and made the conversation all about me—that is disrespectful and basically screams that I'm not ready to graduate to bigger gigs. I was oozing BULLSHIT MONEY ENERGY out of every single pore, and there is nothing that makes a person less likeable. Why would someone with BME like Gordon want to work with a snotty little fuck like me?

---

*Fast-forward a decade, and I now know that Gordon was actually being incredibly generous with his assessment of me.

BULLSHIT MONEY ENERGY: DON'T STEP IN IT

We've all encountered someone with Bullshit Money Energy—they are ego-driven, self-centered name droppers who do things like bark out ridiculous demands and think that acting like a dick makes them powerful. This is the polar opposite of BME. If you are NOT a certified genius on the level of Steve Jobs—who has reinvented the entire world and so it doesn't matter whether or not you're enjoyable to be around—then you can't act horribly and still experience great success. If you want to make a lot of money, people actually have to *like working with you*.

I was twenty-six years old when I was cast on *Million Dollar Listing New York*, and I had not yet learned the lesson that being authentic, kind, and likeable is an important component to success. I wasn't a barbarian by any means; my parents raised us to have manners and to be polite, but I was on a TV show watched by millions of people where acting crazy, loud, and outrageous (and frankly, some of my behavior was downright disrespectful) brought more attention. I will never, ever forget the first time I was recognized by someone for being on TV. I was rushing to the subway one morning when I heard a woman say, "Hey, are you the guy on that show?" I was in a hurry, but I stopped because after an entire year of being on *MDLNY*, no one had ever said anything! I couldn't believe it! When I turned to say, "Yes! It's me!" the woman looked at me like I had kidnapped her little sister and burned down her grandmother's home. Disgust radiated from her eyes like laser beams, and that's when she shouted out: "YOU'RE SUCH A JERK!"

At the time that stung, a lot, but now I understand why she said it. I might not have been a total jerk in real life (I swear I wasn't! ask my friends! ask my mom!), but the qualities I projected in the early seasons of the show didn't exactly make me seem like the kind of guy you'd want to invite to your birthday party.* If you want to really hear the honest truth about what you're like as a person, try going on TV to be judged by millions of people around the globe. And those millions of people made it very clear to me: I was full of Bullshit Money Energy.

Being on reality TV is like living your life under a powerful microscope. I AM NOT COMPLAINING! Being on *MDLNY* has been great for my career and it's really fun! But imagine what it would be like if an entire year of your life was edited down towards your most dramatic (and sometimes ugliest) moments, and then broadcast to the world. Like that time you flipped out because you burned your grilled cheese, or when you lost your temper and cussed like a sailor on the street because you spilled coffee all over yourself on the way to an important meeting. Or that time you were on a date and got a *li'l* drunk. If that was shown as the story of your life, you might end up looking bananas. I *agreed* to have my life filmed (and potentially look bananas on TV), so I was definitely opening myself up to being called a jerk by a total stranger. But after that encounter I started getting noticed in public more often, and then before I knew it, it felt like every other person on the street knew who I was. I had no idea how many people watched the show, and it was

---

*I was more like the guy you'd talk to at a party and then want to throw a drink in his face.

pretty weird! It felt like half of the population really liked me and the other half really, really didn't. Random guys would shout out to me on the street: "Hey, Ryan! You're the man!" *Me?* Oh, I assure you I am not THE MAN. But this made me think—how *did* people see me? And was this how I really wanted to be seen? It's one thing to be disliked for being on a reality television show, but it's another to be disliked in real life. Was what I believed to be a charming Ryan Reynolds–style banter actually making me seem like an asshole? When *Million Dollar Listing New York* started, I wasn't thinking about being liked—I wanted to be a successful broker with a big personality. I didn't understand that those two things were very closely related. How could I make a lot of money in my field if people hated me? You don't hire someone you think is a jerk to sell your home or find you a new place to raise your children! If I wanted to be the best real estate broker in the universe, and make millions doing that, I needed to care more about how I came off to people. I needed to be more comfortable showing my real self and get rid of the overdramatized cartoon of a twenty-something bachelor who acts like it's funny to forget the names of women he dated, or to take off his shirt and jump in the pool at his colleague's open house.

Bullshit Audit

Aside from a handful of exceptions (mainly geniuses), you will not experience massive success if you aren't self-aware. Now that I'm in a position to build a company and hire people, I can tell you I've seen *some things*. I've had brokers who mistakenly think that over-the-top saccharine sweetness or empty invites to their home in the Hamptons is how you endear yourself to a client and land the expensive listings.

It comes off as fake and people see right through that kind of insincerity.

There was a really smart member of my team who had a lot to contribute who had no idea that his colleagues viewed him as standoffish and unhelpful. This definitely could have prevented him from getting ahead and increasing his earning potential.

I've interviewed people for positions who walk into my office with bravado, only to throw themselves in a chair and sit there slumped over and looking sad. If I'm thinking, Are you going to cry? I'm definitely not going to hire you. There's no way you're going to earn big if you're spending all your time searching for tissues to dab away at your tears.

Then there are the people who can't make eye contact. They're staring at the space right above my left shoulder. What are they looking at? Is there a ghost standing behind me?

There are the quiet talkers, the loud talkers (I admit I fell into this category). There's the limp handshake and its reverse, the vice-like death grip (a red flag for BSME, by the way).

You need to know how you come off to others if you want to succeed. Until I was broadcasted to 25 million people, I thought I knew myself, but I was very, very wrong. But I'm about to tell you something very important, so listen closely. If you're not getting what you want from life, if you're not making as much money as you think you should, it's entirely possible that it's because of SOMETHING YOU ARE DOING THAT YOU DON'T EVEN KNOW YOU DO.

CODE #5

Insist on brutally honest feedback. Demand it!
And appreciate how the short-term pain
will promote long-term growth in YOU.

Figuring out whether or not you are likeable starts with being open to criticism. Criticism can be your very best friend. As someone who has opened themselves up to *constant* criticism by being on television and social media—I say bring it. If I'm doing something that is off-putting, offends people, makes me sound dumb, or just drives people crazy, I WANT TO KNOW ABOUT IT. If I've been running around Manhattan all day in the July heat and I come back to the office and someone tells me that I smell, my reaction is not going to be "Why are you so mean?" It's going to be "Oh my God. I had no idea I was so pungent today. Thank you for bringing this to my attention before I went to my next listing pitch!" To be truly successful, you can't respond to feedback and criticism by being defensive. That's what people with Bullshit Money Energy do. Be open to areas where you can be even better! And how will you really know what those are if you DON'T LISTEN TO CRITICISM?

After my failed meeting with Gordon Murray, I asked one of my good (and very honest) friends to give me a quick bullshit audit. How did I come off to people? What did people see when I walked into a room? Scott said, "Ryan, your posture is terrible. It's like you don't even know that being tall is a good thing. You sit slouched over and that makes you look bored." *Really?* I did not know this! But wait, he wasn't finished. Lucky me! "And you don't always look people in the eye when you talk to them either. You look at the ground. Why do you do that? It's strange." I slowly sat up straight, growing about six inches in the process. *Wow, he's right.* I had no idea that I was a sloucher who didn't make eye contact! I'd never get the opportunity to work with big developers (where the potential to earn money was huge) if I looked bored, slouched over, and couldn't make eye contact. The picture I was presenting was not I WILL SELL THE SHIT OUT OF YOUR BUILDING AND MAKE YOU TONS OF MONEY; apparently it was I'm bored and I want to go home—and *that's bullshit.*

The best thing about a bullshit audit is that it can show you things about yourself that can easily be corrected. Ask a few people you trust what your best and worst qualities are. You can take it! What if you eat like an animal? What if you're a loud chewer? Wouldn't you want to know about this before your next business lunch? You do not want to be THAT GIRL WHO CHEWS LOUD. These are small changes that can make a massive difference and greatly improve how you come off to people.

The feedback you get from a bullshit audit are directions for how to transform the raw material that is you into a better, more successful, richer version of yourself! I LOVE feedback and criticism, especially at work. I think of it as my customers literally telling me how I can make more money! Yes, tell me what I can do better!

People with BME pay attention to all of the feedback we get, and it goes into one of two categories. First, there are Valid Points—these are comments that cause us to sit up and pay attention because we want to preserve our bottom line. When customers bring up valid points, we seriously consider if we need to change or alter our practices. For example, do you forget to do things your clients ask you to do? Do you come to meetings unprepared? Do you exaggerate? Do you bring negative energy into the office because it makes YOU feel good to bring others down? Those traits are seriously problematic, and no one will want to hire you. You'll end up with the scraps of low-paying jobs.

And then there are Get-a-Life Points. These are comments you have to be prepared to brush off. They range from "I think all the text on your website should be orange" to "You should be doing business in Panama if you want to be a real success" to "Your feet are weird. Fix them." These are outlier comments. They are incredibly subjective, and either don't have a direct impact on our bottom line or are something we cannot change. My feet are my feet. What can I do? Get a life, foot hater!

CODE #6

Ignore all noise that's not beneficial to you.
It's not raining if you don't get wet.

Seen + Heard + Remembered

If there was a magical charisma pill, I'd take it. Daily. Some people are born with charisma (lucky) and others (like me) are not. When I think of charisma, I think of people like Tom Hanks, Lebron James, and the Dalai Lama. Charisma ultimately means that you are next-level likeable. People who are charismatic have such pull that they can inspire devotion in others; charismatic people *have influence*. Don't you think it would help you to earn more coins if your clients liked you so much they were devoted to you? Charismatic people are able to get their ideas heard and executed, get the right people to call them back, and influence their staff to work hard and do their absolute best work. With this kind of influence, you'd be enjoying success left and right and earning a bundle!

And fortunately, in the adult world, being popular and likeable doesn't have anything to do with being captain of the football team or head cheerleader.

We can all tackle the likeability basics . . . smile more, listen carefully to people—seriously, don't look at your phone! Be curious about life and other people and exude positivity. No one wants to talk to the person whose conversational repertoire ranges from sick cats to crazy ex-girlfriends.

The likeability basics help if you don't have the physical magnetic pull of Brad Pitt or Charlize Theron (and that includes most humans). But there is a simple, easy secret to being instantly more likeable and getting what you want.

At the end of the day people want to be

Seen + Heard + Remembered.

Remember that. Write it down. Tattoo it even.

Starting a conversation with a stranger isn't easy, and I know this will never, ever be my greatest skill, but the Seen + Heard + Remembered (SHR) formula helps, and it makes people feel good!

If I see someone standing alone at a party, I'll walk up to them and say something like:

"Hi. I'm Ryan. Cool purse!" (*THEY'RE BEING SEEN.*)

"Do you live here in New York City?"

"Yeah, close enough. Weehawken."

"Oh, New Jersey is really nice. What do you like about it?" (*THEY'RE BEING HEARD*.)

"I love having the space. I actually keep three beehives in my backyard, and that's okay in Jerz!"

"Wowzers! You're a beekeeper!" (Now *THEY'RE MEM-ORABLE*. This will help you remember them and, who knows, this may be a well-connected person who you'll benefit from knowing for years!)

Until that charisma pill exists, I will use the Seen + Heard + Remembered formula to make positive connections with people. Get those three parts of the formula down in any conversation, and you're golden.

Anyone who read my first book knows that I am obsessed with Follow-up. If follow-up were an Olympic sport, I would be standing on top of the podium with a gold medal around my neck every single time. Try to beat me! And SHR makes it easy and fun to follow up with people. And people turn into new clients, clients turn into MONEY.

The next time I email that person from "Jerz," I'm definitely going to ask about her bees and use it as a conversation starter. Does the queen have a name? Do you have one of those badass beekeeping outfits? Does it scare your neighbors? Remember—I don't personally have to have an intense, personal interest in bees, but I care about Debbie and what my connection to her might bring me. So, I ask her questions I know she will be excited to answer, in part because she will be blown away that I remembered her bees! We all love to be remembered! Debbie the beekeeper of NJ may have three kids who need a place to live in the city, and THERE I AM. Now that brief conversation I had about bees is turning into profits. Or maybe Debbie and her husband will want a pied-à-terre, or maybe their friends will. Being likeable is a HUGE asset when it comes to getting clients, working with clients, and in the end . . . making lots of money. While your bank account balance is shooting to the sky because your likeability is bringing in tons of business, you should know that these same traits can save you money too.

Get People Who Don't Work for You *to Work for You*

A huge part of earning lots of money involves properly utilizing your resources. And there is one important resource that is often overlooked—HUMANS.

Success is never a sole operation, and we are often dependent on other people like receptionists, assistants, bookkeepers, and accountants who are often gatekeepers to something crucial. They technically may not work for you, but think of this crew as a secret network of folks who play a big, but behind the scenes role in sealing your deal. I want the people who cut commission checks to be motivated to do their jobs, I want assistants to put my calls through to their high-net-worth bosses I want to sell apartments to. None of these people work FOR ME. I have zero authority over the assistants of the developers I work for! NONE! But if I have an offer on an apartment and I need to talk to their boss ASAP, I want them to grant me access rather than add my name to a long list of people who called. The faster I close a deal, the more time I save and the more money I make. That's why you need to keep gatekeepers on your side: to put you at the top of the list—to *want* to do things for you . . . *because they like you.* I always recognize the importance gatekeepers have in my life, and I show them appreciation whenever I can.

Other people often play small but important roles in your success, and to ensure you get the help you need when you need it, take control of the relationship in a positive way. If the assistant at your company doesn't tell you when packages arrive, but you NEED the items to plan for an important photo shoot—take control. Buy her lunch, bring cupcakes on her birthday with a card that says, *Thanks for everything you do.* She's fielding calls all day long, managing lots of tasks! If you can get your work done faster and tackle your next project quicker with her help (you just need those packages!), isn't it worth it to develop that relationship? You want your commission checks sent out lightning quick? Develop that relationship. Toss the bookkeeper an email when his favorite baseball team wins a game! "Great game tonight, man!" He'll love that you value his happiness. Getting things done faster with the help of other people enables you to do more and earn more.

A word of warning. Use kindness as a bridge to *strengthen* the relationship—do NOT use it only when you want a task done. BULLSHIT MONEY ENERGY is following up with an immediate ask—saying, "Wow, I love your new bag, where did you get it?" and before you get an answer, you're barking out a list of things you need RIGHT NOW. I promise that document you need mailed is getting shoved right to the bottom of a very large pile before you even turn around, and what's worse? You've burned that bridge. Now, even if you do have a genuinely nice thing to say to that person another day, they'll just assume it's because you need something and will just brush you off. You'll think they're mean to you, when really—it's all your fault. Another thing is, if you're being difficult—own it. If I'm asking for a publicist, designer, or contractor on a project to go above and beyond for me, I'll say, "Thank you for putting up with me. I know I'm asking for a lot and I'm not the easiest. I appreciate everything you're doing." And I'll be sure to express gratitude when the smallest of tasks is accomplished on my behalf. Sometimes I'll email their boss and say, "Wow, Mary is knocking it out of the park. She's awesome!" That results in Mary's boss being happy and funneling that compliment down to Mary, who is going to be less annoyed with me for being so persistent. Gatekeepers are working with many, many more people than just you—so be the easiest, most appreciative person to work with. It gets things done, and that is a huge contribution to your success! But while kindness and generosity are fantastic tools you can use to get more done, they're unfortunately not the approach everyone takes. Sometimes you step in bullshit.

When You Step in a Pile of Bullshit

It's unavoidable. Sometimes you have no choice but to deal with someone who is full of bullshit.

Last year I worked on a deal for a $10 million apartment in the West Village. A guy had come to my open house without a broker and loved the place and wanted to make an offer. Great! The next day his broker, who I didn't even know was part of the deal, reached out to me, and his Bullshit Money Energy was so strong I could smell it *through the phone*. Instead of saying something along the lines of "Thanks for showing the apartment yesterday. Sorry I couldn't be there.

81

But I'm so glad my client loved the apartment, I'm looking forward to getting a deal done," he announces: "I'M TAKING OVER. I'M HANDLING IT. I'LL TAKE CARE OF IT. NOTHING WILL BE DONE WITHOUT ME BLAH BLAH BLAH" *So much bullshit.* It's like he had walked into a prison and started throwing punches to show what a huge tough guy he was. I've encountered this brand of "I'M HOT SHIT" BSME many times, and it's maddening.

When faced with this you might be tempted to toss some bullshit back in their direction, but that only results in shit being thrown all over the fucking place and you're left with a hot, steaming, disgusting mess. You will be covered in shit—and people who are dripping in shit do not win at life. The only way to get rid of the stench of "I'M HOT SHIT" BULLSHIT is to clean up their pathetic little droppings and leave calm and kindness in their place. Get the deal done, get away from them ASAP, and laugh all the way to the bank.

I'M HOT SHIT energy is the absolute worst, but I've developed a few tactics for quick and easy cleanup. First, you must recognize that people often shit in the wrong place because of insecurity. A person with BSME is probably inexperienced and worried about messing up. Spend a couple of minutes researching the bullshitter so you can finish the deal, make your money, and get the hell away from this guy as quickly as possible. He did one deal nine years ago? Bring that up—"Dude, that deal was awesome. I'm so excited to work with you." The recognition and compliment can result in less shit being smeared around while you're forced to work with this guy. You know who else shits in their pants? BABIES. Sometimes the only way to get yourself away from the mess quickly is to let them feel like they've won. You may have used every trick you have in the book to get a job done, but if you want to get PAID, swallow your ego, thank them for their contributions—and sit back knowing full well that you got what you wanted in the end. Let them walk away thinking their shit doesn't stink when it's obvious to everyone that *it does*.

The other form of BSME is more insidious—you can't necessarily smell it right away. You'll be well into an exciting project when the behavior of the person you're working with starts to emit an unpleasant odor. When I'd graduated to selling bigger properties, I was working on a townhouse on the Upper West Side—it was priced at $16 million and was a fantastic listing for me to have in my inventory. But shortly after we started working on this classic, impeccably restored brownstone owned by a wealthy, classy older gentleman, my bullshit meter went off. This guy started calling me six, seven, eight times a day. If I didn't answer right away, he'd get mad and follow up with an email: "What's going on with my listing? Why can't I get you on the phone? Are you even doing anything to sell my house? Are you even in this country right now? You're just a reality TV broker and not a real agent, aren't you?"

You have to be careful in these situations, because the danger of this form of BSME is that they will SMOTHER YOU IN SHIT. Their neediness will spread out and infect your entire life—they'll suck up your time, demand your attention and before you know it, you're devoting more attention to this bullshitter than all of your other clients combined. That deal you thought would bring in big bucks is taking so long (thanks to the BSME) that the income you're making will barely be worth this time.

THAT'S THE WORST.

To avoid being smothered in bullshit, I had to set specific ground rules and expectations about how I and my team would be treated. We explained that because we are in fact *busy trying to sell his house,* we are not available to have lengthy telephone conversations five times per day. Our time (our precious, valuable time!) must be respected in order for us to do our job. I brought in my team member Nicole, and explained we'd be working together. If there is something urgent happening and I'm not available—Nicole will be there to handle it.

To train someone who is used to getting his way by smothering people in shit, you have to draw a firm line about what they can and can't do and point out a PLACE WHERE THEY CAN LEAVE THEIR SHIT.

Getting honest with yourself *about yourself* is hard. After that fateful failed meeting with Gordon Murray, I knew I had a choice—I could continue being a poser and a loser real estate agent who rents cheap apartments to other kids like me forever, or I could shed the bullshit and learn to be someone who people actually want to work with. It changed my life for the better, and I'm grateful I learned to embrace self-awareness, even when it meant facing my negative attributes full-on. Goodbye forever to bad posture and my awful, rude behavior on *MDLNY*!

Don't underestimate the power of shedding the bullshit and radiating positivity. It can be a determining factor in

BULLSHIT MONEY ENERGY ALERT

- **The Expert:** "I don't CARE what Bill Gates says, I know way more about personal computers than that guy."
- **The "I've Got This":** "Thanks for doing all the work, but I'm here now and I'll take over with my huge brain and massive ego. Thanks!"
- **The Selective Listener:** "Here, would you like this bowl of shrimp and peanuts? Oh, you just said you're deathly allergic to both? I didn't hear you, but did you say you went to Harvard?"
- **The Interrupter:** Do not even try to speak to him. You won't get the words ou—.
- **The One-Upper:** "It's awesome that you went to Bali for your honeymoon! I plan to take my fiancé to the moon."
- **The Name Dropper:** "Raphael, the chef here, made me the most amazing birthday dinner. The chocolate on my cake was harvested from cocoa picked just for me. The Kardashians were invited but they couldn't make it."
- **The Label Slave:** "I only wear Gucci, LV, Armani, and Givenchy. I just got this Gucci belt yesterday, DO YOU SEE IT?"
- **Mr. or Ms. Sweetness:** You are addressed as "sweetie" or "honey" but never by your real name (they might not know what it is). Upon meeting Mr. or Ms. Sweetness you are fake-invited to dinner/the theater/the circus/a concert/on vacation on their private yacht. The actual invitation will never come, because a lot of what they're saying to you isn't real.

everything from what jobs you get to how much you get paid.

In the end, it's important to realize that you can't always change other people, and you're going to encounter some assholes on your path to success. Instead of trying to combat their BSME, focus on your level of likeability, earn lots of money, and WIN at life . Stay committed to operating on a higher level. That's Big Money Energy, and it will make you a force in getting everything you want. That's why you're reading this right now, isn't it? To learn how to get more of what you want? You can use this aspect of BME to inspire people, show how capable you are, and make smart, powerful, and interesting people want to be part of your awesomeness. You are already attractive to other people— you just have to stop hiding it! And let's all face it—that's much better than spending your career constantly trying to wash off the shit.

CHAPTER 5

THIS IS HOW YOU DOMINATE

We've all encountered the Dominator. They're that ultra-attractive, well-dressed person whose look is so amazing it basically says, *I am the leading lady/man of my own damn story . . . so stand back please!* Their confidence is so next-level that you automatically assume they're the CEO of a huge company or an up-and-coming film star. The Dominator is stylish, in charge, and their outfit screams I MAKE A LOT OF MONEY so loudly that everyone else is wondering, *How can I get some of that?* You aspire to be like them because they've obviously cracked the code for getting rich, but you hate them (a little, admit it) because you've convinced yourself you can never be like them, and so it's unfair they even exist. The Dominator knows how to capture everyone's attention with their put-together and moneyed look—whatever it is they're wearing . . . a suit, a tuxedo, a dress, a gown, or even a leopard-print kimono says, *I have money and power.* The Dom is like that beautiful but *ultra-expensive* item that catches your eye at the store. You don't take the item home with you, but that doesn't mean you stop thinking about it. The Dominator makes a lasting impression from the moment he or she steps into a room. You know her? You've seen her at the last networking event you attended?

The main point is, more often than not the Dom usually looks . . . expensive.

No one wants to say that, but it's true.

Think of a Dom you may know right now. He looks like an item on a shelf that you can't afford yet. Please understand that as the guy whose look could once be described as "Walmart Cowboy," I'm not judging. I'm here to help by pointing out something simple that could be a huge problem for you.

Listen, we can all pretend it doesn't matter what clothes you choose to wear each day, but it does. I'm sorry to break this news to you, but your appearance—and more specifically your clothing—is important if you want to rule at work, negotiate raises, get promoted, nail job interviews, or have your ideas heard all the time because *you're so awesome.*

So, if you want to get up in the morning and throw on any old T-shirt and a pair of jeans that are crumpled up on your floor because that's what "successful" people on Instagram wear to work, then go right ahead. But hear me out: your favorite concert T-shirt is sending a specific message about who you are. That message could be anything from "I'm a Belieber" to "I am on vacation and really enjoying myself." And that's fine—sometimes (like when you're at home reading this book on your sofa!), but if you want to make more money, your favorite sweats are not doing you any favors.

I know you're probably thinking, "But wait, didn't Mark Zuckerberg mostly wear hoodies? He's worth billions!" Sure, if you are a genius who is changing the world and can drop out of Harvard, and you're absolutely certain you can take your tech company public for billions of dollars while wearing a sweatshirt and a beanie . . . then by all means go for it.* But for everyone else who is not at Harvard, who didn't get a perfect score on the SATs, who wasn't born rich, and who is just working hard to make their dreams become a reality, then you need to understand that what you wear—your first physical impression of yourself to the world—is an expression of your worth in whatever field you work in.

The clothes you choose are a representation of your personal brand. Your outfit is like an ambassador representing who you are, what you believe in, and how much expertise and power you have, before you ever open your mouth. And you have a choice—do you want to look forgettable? Or do you want TO DOMINATE?

I'm writing this in my apartment while wearing a pink tank top and camouflage gym shorts, so I'm not going to pretend that I'm some kind of style guru. But I've experienced firsthand what happens when you accept that the world isn't going to embrace you for your skills, intelligence, or talent if you look like you just crawled out of bed. You may remember that early in my career, I had put together what I called my "nice" outfit. It was a button-down shirt, a pair of khakis, a belt with a very large and shiny

---

*And please email me to buy an apartment! Ryan@RyanSerhant.com!

buckle—all finished off with a pair of cowboy boots. *Yee-haw*. In retrospect, that outfit would have been perfect if I were selling tractors. I'd wake up in the morning, put on that outfit, and head out to work to sell real estate thinking, I hope I get some calls today. It's been slow and I have to pay my electricity bill. Just like my outfit, my hopes and desires were lackluster and generic. A lazy outfit translates into a lazy attitude and lazy energy. It does not show value—it shows that you'll settle for a pile of crumbs. Ask yourself right now, DO YOU WANT CRUMBS? I didn't think so! YOU WANT TO BE THE CRUNCHY TOPPING ON THE CRÈME BRÛLÉE! Even if I had been the most savvy, sophisticated, and experienced broker around (I promise you I wasn't), all of that knowledge and expertise would have been covered up by the outfit I wore.

My outfit clearly said to clients, *I didn't try too hard with life today, but I can find you a cheap apartment and if you throw me some extra cash, I might even help you move in.*

Can you believe I still wondered why I couldn't land seven- and eight-figure clients?

KNOW YOUR AUDIENCE

One of the biggest mistakes I made when I was starting out in sales was not dressing for my audience. I was dressing *for me*—I was wearing what I had in my closet, clothes that felt comfortable. As long you dress like a typical twenty-something, you'll like attract a typical twenty-something, and they likely won't be able to provide the money or opportunity you're seeking for your Big life. Or you'll attract adults stuck in a twenty-something mindset, and they are not typically the people closing big money deals or, for me, buying multimillion-dollar apartments. To attract the right client, I had to get myself in front of a totally different audience made up of people who could afford seven-figure homes. I had never played to an audience like this before, and I knew they would have different expectations about what success looked like. "Let's grab a beer" was not a message that was going to resonate with the audience *I wanted*. If I wanted to get attention from the right audience, I had to know what their symbols of success looked like.

CODE #7

If you want people to take you seriously,
start by looking like someone
who should be taken seriously.

I wanted clients who had a lot of money. Manhattan is the land of well-cut suits, expensive handbags, designer shoes, and watches that cost more than your average college education. In my case, figuring out how to dress wasn't exactly a mystery of epic proportions, and it didn't have to cost a lot of money. So to start, I went to Chinatown.

Chinatown is one of the most bustling neighborhoods in New York City. It's where you go to eat delicious food or buy a fake designer watch on the street. When I was working on my Big Money Energy look, I wanted a symbol of success that would make me look like I was very, *very* expensive. I wanted something I could physically put out there to show the world before I even spoke: *I'm the guy who can sell massive apartments to billionaires.* It seems kind of silly now, but I went to Chinatown and stood on the street hoping I wouldn't run into anyone I knew while I weighed the pros and cons of various fake watches. I went with a Rolex. For a while, that cheap, yellow knock-off watch was like my secret security blanket. Seeing "Rolex" whenever I checked the time was like having a vision board for success right there on my wrist. Eventually, I didn't need the faux-Rolex to make me feel successful (it would also leave a weird green stain on my wrist every time I wore it), but I was grateful it helped me when I needed it most.

The signals for success in my industry are very, very clear. I realize that the expectations and needs vary massively by profession—and not everyone has to wear a suit (LUCKY YOU!). But even if you don't work in a typical corporate setting or your job doesn't give you a dress code, it doesn't mean that you shouldn't create one for yourself.

Whether you're a creative, baker, or hair stylist,* clothes are a tool that can be used to help you exude confidence and experience (even if you have very little). And wouldn't you prefer your look to say "I'm in charge here and I'm doing a fantastic fucking job" rather than "I'm just trying to make it through the day"?

---

*Maybe firefighters and astronauts are exempt from this. If you are dealing with raging fires or you work in outer space, then really you should get a free pass.

The Dom Dress Code

In the beginning of my BME journey I would have had to sell an organ (maybe several) to pay for a Tom Ford suit and a pair of Prada loafers. Okay, so I couldn't wow potential clients with bespoke Savile Row threads, but I developed a few rules that kept me looking BME worthy as I was figuring out what worked best for me—and it works for absolutely any budget.

Fit

Have you ever gotten down on the floor, sucked in your stomach, and held your breath while you slowly eased up a zipper on a pair of pants and thought, "Oh, good! They fit!" Then it takes you twenty minutes to get off the floor because your pants are so tight that you can't move? That is not FIT! It took me years to understand that just because I could button a shirt *did not mean it really fit*. You know when you're out shopping for clothes and you've rejected ten different things because they look terrible—then you put on that one piece and you look in the mirror and think, "Goddamn, I make this shirt look good." HELLO, IT'S BECAUSE THAT ITEM "FITS" YOU PROPERLY. While literal fit is important, that's not the kind of fit I'm talking about.

BME fit is about finding clothes that emphasize your best qualities and deflect attention from the parts you're less excited about. I'm forever on the search for pants that don't make my legs look like skinny bananas. For me to get the right fit I also need long shirts (because my torso is so long) that are also a super-slim fit. I've found one brand of shirts that exists for my proportions, and so they're all I buy.

Back when I had little money, I had to make do with whatever I could find on the clearance rack, which was okay! The only suits I could afford were often a little boxy and loose, and I looked like a teenager who'd borrowed his dad's suit (the complete opposite of BME), but I made it work. Once I found a tailor and he used his magic to make my suits fit; he transformed a less than impressive suit into something that looked fantastic. Tailors are geniuses. Find a good one who doesn't cost you too much (most dry cleaners will do tailoring for cheap), and watch your wardrobe improve and your life change.

Clean

I know wearing clean clothes sounds obvious. We all know we should not go to work wearing the old college T-shirt we wash only now and then. But when I was first starting out, clean meant something different than not wearing clothes from the bottom of the dirty laundry pile. My clothes were *literally clean*, but to give off Big Money Energy I became meticulous about wrinkles, lint, and pet hair (there was a brief period in my life when I had a pet pig*). The handheld steamer is my best friend, and to this day I always have a lint roll handy. Before getting dressed I gave my clothes a once-over for an errant smoothie stain or a piece of string dangling from the sleeve of my otherwise ultra-clean and well-fitting dress shirt. I wasn't going to give off Big Money Energy if I was sitting in a meeting thinking, Can everyone tell that my pig slept on my pants?

---

*Yes, pigs actually do have hair.

When I was on a tight clothing budget, I went for simple lines and neutral colors—I stayed away from things like bold colors, plaids, and stripes until I had a better understanding of what I could pull off and could buy higher-quality pieces. Clean is safe when it comes to clothes, and there is nothing wrong with that. If you look messy, people will assume YOU are messy—your work, your personality, and your mind. So, clean up.

Shined

What you choose to put on your feet can say a lot about who you are. This goes for both men and women. When I was ready to go DOMINATOR, I invested in a solid pair of classic-looking loafers. They complemented whatever I was wearing, and I kept those loafers looking *pristine*. Fast-forward a bit into the life of baby BME Ryan, and those shoes eventually had holes in the soles courtesy of the mean streets of Manhattan. Whenever it rained or snowed, I could look forward to having soaking-wet feet . . . but no one ever knew that because I kept them perfectly shiny on top. Like hair gel, shoe polish can take you further than you think, and I certainly wasn't going to let people know my shoes were literally falling apart.

Shoes are like the crowning glory of your outfit. And that means the shoes you put on can ruin a perfectly good outfit. Basic *but shined* shoes trump trashed designer shoes every time! Have you ever seen a super-impressive person in a killer outfit with scuffed-up, worn-down shoes? You haven't—because that's not how you DOMINATE.

I went through an unfortunate phase where I wore sneakers with a suit. I thought this would make me look hip and cool because I saw other people doing it. *Check out my cool kicks paired with my classy suit! Business on top, Saturday on bottom!* Danielle, our producer on *MDLNY*, would say things like, "Oh, that's what you're wearing? Interesting choice, Ryan." It became clear she wasn't saying so much that I had made a unique style choice; it was that I had made a bad choice based on how the outfit looked on *me*. I didn't look cool. I looked confused, like I got dressed in the dark and threw on whatever shoes I could find with my hands. Some people can really pull off the fabulous suit with cool sneakers combo—I, however, cannot. Know thyself.

Listen to what I'm about to tell you! Don't ruin a fabulous dress by tossing on flip-flops! Don't wear your gym shoes with a suit unless that's a look you can really own. And don't wear shoes that call attention to your feet—that's attention your face and your personality will lose. I went through a phase where I wore really pointy dress shoes. They looked like men's witch shoes. I had so many pairs of them. They were in fashion for a bit, and while I thought the attention I got from them was great, I realized people were remembering me more as the real estate guy with pointy shoes than the smart guy who knew a lot about real estate and would be nice to work with.

Clothes that fit and shoes that shine make you feel *amazing,* and that energy shows outwardly in everything you do. Your outfit is also the world's best business card (the use of business cards is fading!)—instead of just handing over a piece of card stock with your name and contact info, your outfit can speak for you: *I know you're going to remember meeting me because it obviously looks like I'm a boss.*

THIS IS HOW YOU DOMINATE

HAVE A CONFIDENCE COSTUME

As you're building your Dominator look and determining what works best for you, have one really fantastic outfit. This is your confidence costume. Today my Dominator-wardrobe game is TIGHT. It helps me look successful, accomplished, polished, and confident. But for those really big meetings or closings, I still have a couple of go-to outfits that make me feel amazing. My all-time favorite is a navy-blue suit with a white shirt, a pink Hermès tie, brown Lanvin shoes, and my AP watch that I saved up for over a year to buy (turns out I was never really a Rolex kind of guy). Whenever I put this outfit on, a transformation takes place. I feel like I can tackle anything. I have one other outfit that makes me feel equally incredible. It's a black pinstripe suit that I wear with black Prada shoes and a Louis Vuitton belt—no brand logos showing, but the quality is unmistakable. Just try to mess with me in this outfit—*you can't.* I'm invincible.

As you're building your wardrobe and your BME, focus on creating one super-charged, amazing outfit that makes you feel like a Dominator. You'll feel its power every time you put it on.

I was fired from a big building once, and I thought the developer hated me. But when asked during an interview years later how it was to work with me, she said, "Ryan was great. Fun, smart, great energy, and a great dresser. I knew people would buy from him the moment I saw him." True story. She still fired me though.

I love my Dominator clothes—but I love the moment when I morph back into regular Ryan even more. After a full day of meetings, pitches, phone calls, and hopefully

---

CODE #8

Don't dress for your mood today;
dress for the success you want tomorrow.

---

lots of deal making, I walk out of the elevator and into my apartment. I take off my shoes (New York City streets are gross), kiss Emilia and Zena, say hi to Yiayia, and then march directly into the bedroom where I shed my Dominator uniform and replace it with my favorite pink tank top and sweat shorts. Broker Ryan talks a mile a minute, and regular Ryan is definitely quieter, but I'm still the same confident, successful guy who just left his Prada shoes at the door. Thanks to BME, I've reached a place in my life where I'm still the same no matter what I have on. June Shen wore the same track suit every day with me for a week while looking at $2–$3 million apartments, but she wore it with confidence and an attitude that said, "I'm the one with the millions, so I'm going to be comfortable while jet-lagged." Remember that someday, ideally in the near future, your BME will shine bright no matter what you are wearing. You'll have the right clothes you need to conquer your goals, but at the end of the day when you change back into your comfy clothes, that energy will stick with you. Because it is who you are now.

YOU ARE WHAT YOU DON'T EAT

Let's talk about the most obvious form of energy—the food you eat. You won't feel good about what you wear on the outside if you don't feel good on the inside. I should know. I was an overweight kid who was addicted to chocolate pudding for years. Now I only eat food between 12 p.m. and 6 p.m. every day. Some days if I feel like it, I'll fast for twenty hours just because I can. I don't let this plan stop me from having a dinner out either (with my lovely wife or with clients). If I know I have a dinner date, I don't start eating until 2 p.m. Since I started doing this I've found I have more energy, and I'm happier. I wake up at 4 a.m. full of BME and ready to dominate.

A company called Food Matters prepares all of my food for me the night before, and delivers it to my apartment every morning. If you were to look in my lunch box you'd likely find egg bites, fruit, a protein smoothie, a lean meat and vegetables, and a healthy snack. It's all good and I love that I literally DO NOT HAVE TO THINK ABOUT WHAT I'M GOING TO EAT. It's all right there in my giant lunch box. Once you manage what you do and don't eat and when, you'll find that you have much more control over your mood, your physical appearance, and your energy. Add a good-fitting outfit on top of that, and you're dominating.

CHAPTER 6

THE ART OF SELECTIVE COMMUNICATION

I met Sebastian, aka the International Man of Mystery,* when I sold him a $17 million apartment after six years of follow-up with no response (till death do I stop following up). Now, Sebastian was ready to add a trophy property to his real estate portfolio: a Hamptons estate. The purchase of his Hamptons house would prove equally tricky. Many times, when a deal falls apart it's due to a breakdown in communication—there isn't enough of it! People aren't talking! This deal was different; it only worked because there was a certain piece of information I kept close to my chest after careful consideration. I knew my client wanted this house (and I certainly wanted my commission), but this piece of information was so ABSURD I knew sharing it

---

*You know, like the guy in the Dos Equis commercials? "He has a charm so contagious they made a vaccine for it. . . . He taught his horse to read his emails for him. . . . His blood smells like cologne. . . . He is the most interesting man in the world!" If you want to know how we met, you'll have to read *Sell It Like Serhant*.

would unleash a battle of egos unlike anything I had ever seen. It had to be handled with kid gloves . . . or billionaire gloves.

The Hamptons technically consists of a bunch of beach towns on the southeastern shore of Long Island, but this isn't your typical beach vacay town. In the Hamptons if you pop out for froYo with chocolate-covered gummy bears, you may be standing in line in front of Rhianna. And oh, is that Jerry Seinfeld getting coffee? *Yes, it is.* The Hamptons is the 90210 of beach vacation spots on the East Coast. It's where celebrities and the ultra-wealthy flock to enjoy the sandy beaches, attend A-list parties, and wait in very, very long lines to eat at restaurants even though they have a chef's kitchen *with an actual chef in it* at home.

As a result of all this super-exclusive summer fun, a charming little cottage in the Hamptons is going to cost you several million dollars. But Sebastian wasn't looking for a cottage—he wanted a full-on oceanfront estate with water views from the master bedroom, a gym, an infinity pool, enough bedrooms to house a basketball team, plus a guest house, a screening room, and another outdoor screening room. His budget for this palace of summer wonder? *About $30 million!* The International Man of Mystery is very busy using his Big Money Energy to earn hundreds of millions of dollars, so he hired me because (a) I'm the best and (b) he trusts me after working together for eight years.

I took a helicopter out to the Hamptons for the afternoon so I could show Sebastian some of the most exclusive properties in the world . . . *over FaceTime.*

Sebastian fell for house number three. An off-market estate with 100 feet of private and perfect beachfront. The

8,000-square-foot interior had recently been renovated to look like a palace. The 6,000 square feet of outdoor deck space spread across three levels had extraordinary views—and if Sebastian got hungry while staring at his enviable view or watching his massive outdoor hurricane-proof TV, it was no big deal because there was also a pizza oven. This property was quietly asking $50 million.

The other properties Sebastian had rejected for not having fireplaces big enough to roast a wooly mammoth or garages that could adequately house his vintage car collection were in the $25–$35 million range, so naturally we offered $28 million for the $50 million house. No response. We upped it to $30 million—the TOP of his budget, he told me. No response. Okay, how about $32 million—"What's another two bucks?" Now they were listening.

But we weren't singing the same song quite yet. We were still $18 million apart after all, and the house wasn't even on the market. After months of negotiations I got a call from the seller's broker: "They aren't going below $40 million—that's $10 million off but here's the thing. They will sell him the house and include every single item that's in it." $40 million was still a lot higher than Sebastian wanted to pay—that's a huge price tag, even if you're the International Man of Mystery. But with everything in it? The house was perfectly designed. Sebastian wouldn't have to spend any money there, and I did a quick calculation in my head. How much money does a billionaire spend on furnishings? You could spend $1 million per room easily if you added up the custom beds, handmade carpets, built-ins, window treatments, gold ceilings, and fountains. I'm not kidding. I caught Sebastian on the phone right before he was about to fly off to Kentucky to buy a pair of pure-bred racehorses.

"Listen, it's $40 million—I know that's more than you wanted to spend. But here's the thing: it will be fully furnished, and I know your time is very valuable to you, so you won't have to spend a second thinking about decorating it. The house is perfectly renovated, it comes with everything from wineglasses to sofas to llama-hair stair runners. So really . . . it's like you're spending $40 million on the house and getting everything in it for free! That's a $10 million savings, not to mention the cost of your time and effort. So, there you go. The perfect beachfront mansion for, net to you, $30 million, just like you asked for." When you're a closer, you know that math can be subjective. Sebastian got quiet.

CODE #9

If you want to convince someone to spend more,
never focus on the money—focus on the VALUE.

He either hated this idea or he was busy doing something else—like signing an agreement to buy a small country. Then he spoke: "Fine."

Here's the thing about billionaires—they're very rarely excited about money. They have so much of it. But he wanted this house and I was delivering it to him. So, begrudgingly, we had a deal! And this is where the communication portion of this story got interesting. Sometimes earning money requires incredibly careful communication. In this case, I felt like I was operating an FBI sting.

KILL HIGHLY CONTAGIOUS PROBLEMS OR DIE

One of the biggest secrets to earning more money is learning to identify and eradicate problems that have the potential to infect your entire deal. Enter the parts of my job you will never, ever see on any of my shows on BRAVO or my vlog on YouTube: The excitement of Land Easements! The thrill that is a Certificate of Occupancy! I'm telling you, a lot of my job is a real grind. There is so much behind the scenes going back and forth before a deal is closed! At last, the final version of the contract for Sebastian's Hamptons house has arrived—we are so close to closing this deal, and I am so close to getting a very large commission check, but then my stomach drops. SURPRISE, BITCH! There's a rider attached to the contract.

> Rider to Clause 16 (a) The following items are excluded from the sale:
> 1. Television in second living room
> 2. Rug in guest house
> 3. Blanket in den

Oh shit. I shout across the office—my voice is so loud I'm sure everyone on the street six floors below can hear me: "YOLANDA, DO NOT SEND THE RIDER TO SEBASTIAN."

I could picture exactly what would happen if Sebastian saw this rider: he'd drop whatever he was doing, pick up the phone, and say in his super-calm and cool voice:

"Ryan. Sure. They can keep their TV, and rug, and their little blanket." Then add: "And I'll keep my $40 million."* *Click.*

I was not going to lose this huge deal I had been working on for months over a rug. I called the seller's broker right away, before this problem could kill everything about this deal in its path.

"Are you serious? You sell my client the house with everything in it and you're now taking stuff back? I don't care how small the items are—it's the idea that you're retrading on us that will KILL this deal. We are giving you $40 million in cash. Your client doesn't get to go shopping in the house he's selling to my client."

The broker told me he'd see what he could do—I knew he didn't want to lose this deal either. He called me back a few minutes later. "Okay, they'll concede on everything, except the blanket. They are not willing to give up the blanket!" *What?* Was this blanket woven from unicorn fur? Did it possess magical powers?

"Listen. I'll buy them a new blanket! Can you get me the details on the blanket, and I'll find the exact same one! Or do they want a better blanket? I'll get them a quilt made by the Amish! I'll do whatever they want! What's their fantasy blanket?" I could not believe this huge deal was coming

---

*I will never, ever understand what goes on in the head of a billionaire. It's like they're a different species.

down to a rich guy's blankie—it's like we were dealing with toddlers.

There was a pause on the phone . . . "Ryan. I'm afraid this specific blanket has sentimental value. They must have the blanket." Was this a joke? How was this happening? How would I possibly explain this to Sebastian?

CODE #10

When a client hits you with a crazy demand,
know it's never about the money;
it's about establishing control.

Here's one thing I've learned: all seemingly innocent problems can fester, infecting everything in their path and eventually killing an entire deal. This was no ordinary blanket. I saw it for what it was: a **Highly Contagious Problem**! These sorts of little problems have to be stopped in their tracks or they can slowly and painfully suck the life right out of you, your deal, and your income. If we were to agree to give them their blanket, it would feed their greed and the demands would start to grow. A Highly Contagious Problem begins with a few interesting symptoms:

Reluctance
The *person* is reluctant to let go.

"Sure, I'll sell you my beloved bicycle, but I really want to keep the seats and the handlebars. Hope you understand!"

Reaction

The *person* has an irrational reaction to a normal request. This reaction is a warning sign of other extreme reactions to come if these symptoms aren't treated. "Why are you insisting that I sell you a bike with the seat and handlebars? Can't you just be happy with a partial bike that you can't even ride?"

Retraction

The *person* is ready to give up the deal. This symptom is hard to cure. The person will continually find a way to back out of the deal and waste your time. You'll never see that paycheck!

––––––––

I knew that if I wanted to save the deal—IT WAS SUCH A HUGE DEAL—I needed to put a stop to this problem immediately. If you learn to identify and treat a highly infectious problem quickly, you will close deals faster and make more money. If I didn't put my foot down, I knew the problem would spread and things would get totally ridiculous: *"Well, we really love the door knocker, it's very special to us so we must keep it."* And who knew where it would all stop? The kitchen towels? A bathtub? Would the deal finally die in a fight about an oven mitt after months of suffering?? I wasn't going to let this blanket kill my commission (and my soul!). If not handled carefully, a Highly Contagious Problem represents the moment when a deal starts to die. Deals that die do not bring you any money! To squash it, I'd have to dish out the cure, the **Three Cs: Calm, Control, and Conviction.**

Calm

People with Big Money Energy know that calm equals power. When I saw the rider in Sebastian's contract, I was not calm (just ask Yolanda, my director of operations, or any person walking along Broadway between Houston and Prince in SoHo that day). It's possible I was crying on the inside ~~a little~~ a lot. But if you want to eradicate a highly contagious problem, take a long breath before you take your next step. Concentrate on the picture you want to present to the other side. Do you want to yell and scream like a maniac? Trust me, that will not contain the infection—it will feed it! To prevail, you need to come off as so calm, and so collected, that there is no weakness for the Highly Contagious Problem to grab on to (which will only increase its power!). Calm = in charge. Make sure your thoughts are clear to you first, make a decision, and then clearly relay your expectations. It's the only way to stay strong and rid yourself of a Highly Contagious Problem.

Control

People with Big Money Energy are not afraid to set boundaries. I knew that if I didn't take control of the situation, the seller's desire for the blanket would turn into a need to keep the toaster. It would spiral out of my control, and I'd be dealing with weird requests for the rest of my life (and never get paid). To contain the infection, I needed to establish a **"no-go zone."** In this case, the interior of the house was the "no-go zone." It was the one area of the negotiations where we would not move, because this deal point had been agreed upon by both parties earlier. This can be painful to the other party, but stick to your guns. "But I love

my blanket! I'll die without it!" they might say, crying croc-
odile tears. However, you can offer a bit of pain relief to
keep the deal healthy. If you are a graphic designer and
your client is saying, "Your fee only entitles me to three designs for the labels of my homemade cat food? I want five!
Cats are special! And I want sketches of all my cats! Can
you make them birthday cards too?"

More than three designs may be your no-go zone, but
perhaps you can offer them something else on *your* terms:
"My fee entitles you to three designs, but yes—cats are
the best and I will also create an adorable cat sticker that
you can include with all your shipments of homemade or-
ganic cat food." People with *BME* set boundaries to contain problems.

Conviction
Conviction is the final but *essential* weapon in the fight
to the death against the Highly Contagious Problem. You
will NOT stand a chance against the problem if you don't
address it firmly. Any wavering on your expectations . . .
whether it's apparent in the tone of your voice, accidently
blurting out a "well, maybe" or "I understand, I'll see what
I can do" is like taping a red flag to your forehead that says:
"I DON'T ACTUALLY MEAN WHAT I'M SAYING, SO GO
AHEAD AND WALK ALL OVER ME." People with *BME*
speak with conviction, not just when squashing problems,
but all the time! I didn't understand how important it was
when I was a kid, but growing up my dad always spoke with
conviction. He owned his ideas, whether they were about
work, a book he liked, or why my brother and I could not
have a video game console. He stated his position clearly

and had facts to back it all up when necessary. Conviction is how people speak on talk shows and on other media platforms! No one wants to watch an "expert" wavering like: "Glow-in-the-dark jumpsuits are definitely going to be the biggest fashion trend this season. Wait. Maybe it will be burlap dresses? Or rainbow tank tops? I'm not really sure now that I think about it." Own your thoughts and ideas and share them with other people! Even if you're wrong or you change your mind later when you get new information, at least you have the courage and the confidence to have an opinion at all times.

KEEP SOME CARDS CLOSE TO YOUR CHEST

I've always taught my team that communication is everything—selling or buying a house can be a stressful and emotional experience. Simply keeping a client up to date on what we're doing on their behalf, why we are making certain decisions, or alerting them to where we are in the process can go a long way towards calming emotions and preventing me from getting text messages at 3 A.M. like:

"Ryan? OMG. Is my asking price TOO low? Why is that the asking price? My next-door neighbor got like $75,000 more and her ceiling isn't painted with rainbows like mine is! SAD EMOJI. ANGRY EMOJI. CALL ME."

Clear and honest communication goes a long way . . . and as I like to say, *it's free*. But part of being a successful businessperson is learning that while you are always honest, there are times when you must be selective about which details you share and which ones you hold back.

The case of the world's most expensive blanket is the perfect example. Had I called my client who was busy buying banks, sports teams, and a rare alpaca to say:

"Hi, how's it going? Well, I'll have those contracts for your Hamptons dream mansion shortly—but just so you know, we're having a fight about a $100 blanket. I'll let you know how it goes!"

No, no, no.

I could kiss that deal, that client, and any referrals he would have given me goodbye forever. And over a lifetime that would add up to a substantial amount of lost income! No thank you!

Sebastian is busy, important, and I'm not going to bother him with those details. People who are high earners know that YOU handle pesky problems so your most lucrative clients never have to worry about them. This requires building the ultimate level of trust. I understand that it can be hard to determine when to share and when to selectively communicate. I tell my team to "**MAP It Out**" when they're trying to figure out if a piece of information is essential— meaning they need to drop everything and call the client now—or if they can handle it on the client's behalf. The MAP CHECKLIST is:

♦ *(M) Material*
  Is this material information? In my world, that means knowing if there is a fact that would cause a buyer or seller to make a different decision. While I know Sebastian would have gone bananas over the blanket scenario, it wasn't a material fact. The blanket did not directly impact the value of the house. If we found out the house

was built over a bubbling pit of lava and could burst into flames at any time—that is material information. Or if the two-floor home your client wants to buy should only have been one floor and the second floor was added illegally—again, this is material information. Or if the renovation was done without permits and was never signed off on by the city, *DROP EVERYTHING AND CALL.*

You need to consider: Is the information you're dealing with directly related to the outcome? Is it crucial to the deal or project you're working on? A material fact can be like life-or-death-level information. If it is, then this is not the time to selectively communicate. If not, keep moving forward without getting your client involved!

♦ *(A) Answer*

Do you have an answer to the problem? Can you envision how this situation will be resolved? I was confident that I could solve the issue with the unicorn-fur blanket. I had dealt with countless bizarre requests over the years, and I knew how to tackle it. But wait, Ryan! What if I don't have an answer?! We've all been there, right? But often that's false thinking. If you don't have an answer *yet*, how can you get one? Seek guidance from someone who has more experience than you. Ask how they would handle it. Or go to one of your smartest colleagues; talk it over and see what kind of answer you can come up with. For Sebastian's deal, I went back and forth with Jen Alese, my director of new development who is a killer negotiator, playing out the scenario every which way to see how I should proceed.

Very early on in my career, I found a rental in a co-op building for a twenty-four-year-old investment banker named Paul. In New York City, co-ops equal rules—it's a totally different process than the rental transactions I had been doing. Deals in co-op buildings involve a board application, tax returns, a personal interview, business references, a personal essay, SAT scores, blood tests, a talent competition, and finally a duel on the rooftop of the building (okay, I'm exaggerating, but only a little). Ultimately, I didn't know what I was doing, and Paul was frustrated because he just wanted to move in! I was frozen, and I didn't know where I'd gone wrong—why wouldn't anyone at the building return my calls? I was paralyzed and made the mistake of not seeking out an answer to the problem, hoping that it would just go away and Paul would be able to move in without any confrontation. I also didn't tell him I was struggling, though I was working on an answer. This situation solved itself when my client called me up to tell me I was the "worst broker in the world" and that he'd made a call and finished the deal himself. If you have an answer to a problem— pursue it. If you don't have an answer, find one before you pick up the phone. Always deliver a problem WITH the solution—otherwise you're a quarterback throwing a pass to no one, and the ball will drop.

♦ *(P) Personality*
Who are you dealing with? Is this client someone who appreciates play-by-play information? We've all worked with people who want to know everyyyything, even if it's something as minor as "I know you like to be filled

in on everything, and just FYI, during the open house today a fly landed on your kitchen counter. I took care of it—none of the prospective buyers saw it, so all's well that ends well!"

If you want the jobs and clients who bring in huge dollars, you have to understand the wants and needs of the people you are dealing with—and everyone is different. What does your gut tell you? Will your client want to know about that pesky fly, or will they think, "Why the hell are you bothering me with something so ridiculous while I'm in Pilates?" Anticipate as much as you can the kind of reaction you'll get before deciding whether to selectively communicate. Know your audience! You're the one who is in control of every conversation and every situation.

If my hair wasn't gray already, Operation BlanketGate would have done the job. In the end, after establishing our no-go area and calmly telling the other broker that the only thing stopping their client from getting the $4 million deposit wired into their account that day was a blanket—they saw the light. From there on, the deal was pretty simple. Sebastian got his contracts without the ridiculous rider, and a few weeks later he got to celebrate the purchase of his insane new beach home with a good scotch by the fireplace, wrapped up in his perfect $40 million throw. I texted him after the closing, asking when I could come to the house and stay for a night. He still hasn't texted me back.

CHAPTER 7

THE 1,000-MINUTE RULE

Do you know what you have in common with Elon Musk, Steph Curry, Jeff Bezos, the Rock, Oprah Winfrey, and J. K. Rowling? You all have the same number of minutes to use however you choose, every single day. Twenty-four hours in a day multiplied by 60 minutes gives all of us 1,440 minutes—take away a reasonable amount of time to sleep, eat, shower, and hug your kids, and you're left with 1,000 minutes. You can use your minutes to conquer the world and earn buckets of money, write books, train for a marathon, hang out with your family, have drinks with friends, buy groceries, meditate, do laundry, watch Netflix, or post pictures of your dog on Instagram. Every day you wake up with a fresh 1,000 minutes in your bank of time. You are the CEO of that bank, and it is totally up to you how to put those minutes to use. You're as rich in time every Monday as Oprah and the *actual* richest man in the world.

You can no longer think of your time as free anymore. Big you—successful you—knows that time is expensive, and when we think about our time like we do our money, we can shift our mindset to not throwing it away. You wouldn't throw away $100 would you? Well, that's what you're doing with an hour and a half when you're not being productive—you're basically throwing your income out the window. Bye-bye, money!

The clock starts ticking the second you wake up, and if you aren't aware of how those precious minutes are being used, it will suddenly be 9 P.M. and you'll be wondering (once again) how you didn't find the time to call back all of your clients or follow up with that new contact you made last week. "The day got away from me." "Such a busy day, I'll do all that tomorrow!" Sound familiar? That's because there are a few common minute killers sneaking around, trying to bankrupt our time bank right under our noses, often without us even knowing! By learning to identify and destroy these minute killers, you can take control of your day, maximize your time, and *make more money*.

Minute Killer #1:
The Perfection Trap

I like to be the first one at work. If I were to waltz in around 11 A.M., kick back and eat a breakfast burrito while listening to a podcast, that sends a clear signal to my team: No rush here! Just show up whenever you want to!

One day I arrived at around 7:30 A.M. (after my daily workout) to find one of my team members already at her computer, hard at work. Good for her! I answered my emails, then was off for a long day of appointments. When I got back to the office around 6:30 P.M., she was exactly where I'd left her. The look of concentration on her face was intense—like she was trying to split the atom.

I returned calls, answered emails and had a meeting, and when I was finally getting ready to leave at 8 P.M. she was still furiously typing away. What has she been doing all this time? I wondered. She must be writing a screenplay at work. I had to ask.

"Hi. You have been working so hard all day! How's it going?"

She took a deep breath. "Yeah. I just really want to get this email to a client perfect, so I'm working really hard on it! I'm pulling as much data as I can. I'm doing all my research. I need to convince him I'm right!"

I couldn't have been more shocked if she'd just told me she was an alien from another galaxy. She's been writing and rewriting the same email all day?

While I appreciate the desire to send flawless communication, *it doesn't matter how perfect anything is if you don't get results.* And how can you be getting results if you're spending twelve hours on one basic task? That's 720 minutes! That's a lot of time + money! She had fallen into the dark, ugly pit known as *Analysis Paralysis*, or the perfection trap. The perfection trap will rip through your 1,000 minutes and leave you broke . . . You were obsessing over one email all day, and now you have no minutes left. You should have saved some to go to that open house your client wanted you to preview in the East Village, and you managed to miss your networking drinks too! Wonder how many amazing potential clients you would have met there? You didn't meet any new people today, and that's your whole job! There's nothing left to do but go home and inhale a peanut butter sandwich and toss the clothes you wore on the floor and pass out in your bed. Well done, Ms. Perfect!

Analysis Paralysis is a disease that keeps many hardworking people from reaching their earning potential. They overanalyze and overthink everything to death, because they believe that time is free and the result of their "hard work" will make them money. That's wrong. Their time is not free and the result is a gamble even if the email *is* perfect. The perfection trap actually costs them MORE money, and they would know that if they just looked at their day like a CEO would look at their company. They would budget the appropriate *funds* for each task at hand, knowing that the only way to make a return on that new 1,000 minutes every day is to be as careful with them as you would with your own cold, hard cash.

If perfectionism gets its grip on you, you'll be wasting one day after another. Stay away from it and instead acquaint yourself with *excellence*. Excellence is real while perfection is a myth. Think about it! Have you ever read an obituary that said: "LAURA WROTE PERFECT EMAILS"?

CODE #11

Perfectionism is like a straitjacket that you need to
break out of if you want to take risks, go bigger,
and succeed on the highest levels.

A life full of excellence includes winning awards, running a successful business, and raising great kids—that's the kind of thing you hear about! Excellence is about having high but achievable standards. Excellence doesn't want to suck the life out of your minutes—excellence wants you to get results. You have two choices. You can go home at the end of a productive day to hang out with your family feeling great because you are *winning at life*. Or, you can make yourself another pathetic sandwich and step over sad piles of clothes so you can fall into bed feeling like shit because you didn't get anything done. *Again.*

Which scenario do you want for your own life?

If you've been known to fall headfirst into the perfection trap, there's a way to keep you out of it. You need to TAG yourself out, and here's how:

♦ *(T) Trust*

Know what you're doing. Overthinking is the gateway to perfectionism! You DO have the skills to execute the task. Don't overthink it: make a plan for conquering this task. Write down your objective and list the steps you need to take to get it done. EXECUTE is your motto from now on. Just like a trader at a big investment bank! You will execute trades with your 1,000 minutes each day.

♦ *(A) Ask*

Talk to someone who knows more than you. This could be a colleague. If you're terrified of making an embarrassing mistake, or you're not sure your presentation is nailing the point home, or there's a problem with that big deal you have in the works, quickly ask a trusted (non-perfectionist) co-worker to provide some feedback. You should have this person on speed dial, and they should be a strong decision maker. And no matter what you do, do NOT ask a fellow overthinker, or the two of you will be trapped on your weird island of perfection together forever—with no way off.

♦ *(G) Give*
Give yourself a time limit. Two minutes for an email, an hour for a PowerPoint presentation. This will train your brain to move through these tasks without draining your minute bank. Every task you do and every action you take costs you time, which costs you money. That extra ten minutes you took that you didn't really need? That just cost you ten bucks. Do you like cutting up $10 bills?

There will be some clear signs that you're climbing out of the perfectionist hole, and those signs will be in the form of MANY RESULTS. Are you flying through your to-do lists? Have you added more to your plate? Are you making more money personally, increasing clientele, or growing profit for your business? If you're not finishing tasks and heading back to the opportunity buffet for second helpings and raking in more dollars, you may still have a problem. TAG yourself until you seriously, actually see the light in the form of GETTING SHIT DONE.

Minute Killer #2:
The Red Zone

Usually open houses are hazard free, but there are occasionally some issues. I've dealt with plenty of dirty shoes leaving footprints on light-colored rugs, fingerprints on glowing appliances that must be wiped away, nosy people poking in closets for far too long, and God help me . . . clogged toilets. But what happened in the apartment on West 22nd Street was a brand new problem.

Heather was spending $5 million on her first home on West 22nd Street, and she wanted to bring her dad along before she finalized this huge purchase. Dad was really being *a dad*—he opened the refrigerator and gazed inside (*what's he doing, looking for sandwich fixings?*). The dishwasher was subject to the same amount of scrutiny. All eight of the burners on the stove were tested and the oven was turned on (*oh my God, how far is he going to take this? is he going to bake a cake?*). I followed him around with a cloth, wiping away his fingerprints like we were in some kind of organized crime ring—*we were never here! You can't prove we touched anything!*

I was polishing the front of the microwave when I heard "What the hell is this?" Dad was pointing to a large but barely visible metal access panel along the wall, where the controls for the HVAC unit were located. The "Meticulous family" who lived in the apartment had hired an artisan to create custom venetian paneling, at great expense, so the panel would blend into their perfect walls and not be a metal eyesore. Before I could explain what it was and ask him to kindly not touch it . . . Dad had ripped the very expensive, artisan-crafted HVAC-panel *off the wall* to inspect what was inside. Precious Italian plaster plummeted to the floor along with my spirit, because this is the kind of unexpected situation that kills my hard work. It's like someone took all the sweat equity I put into the deal, threw it on the floor, crushed it with their foot, and once they were sure all of my efforts were pulverized, they SPIT on whatever was left.

When I told the Meticulous family what happened, they were furious: "Ryan!!! You know how hard it was for us to find an artisan to make that! We had to ship a man in from Italy! We are so mad we can't even think right now!" And guess what? The buyer no longer wanted to spend $5 million on an apartment that was falling to pieces, said her daddy! Goodbye, commission; goodbye, minutes! It was nice knowing you! UGH!

Shit happens at work. Just like everyone else, I have projects and deals that die. For me, this can be anything from getting fired from a listing or a buyer disappearing off the face of the earth, to a client discovering her little dog Fido exceeds the weight limit at the new co-op she just bought.* These are the kinds of problems that can turn my calendar into a RED ZONE.

The Red Zone is a scary and angry place where you will not be bringing in more income, because you will use all of your minutes to put out fires, do damage control, care for disappointed clients who are irate because you left finger-prints behind.

A dog groomer on your staff shaved the wrong dog? Welcome to the Red Zone. You are crushed because you pitched your heart out for a gig, but the client went with

---

*Yes, most buildings in NYC allow dogs . . . but only under a certain weight. This is a real thing. People will put their dogs on diets just like a boxer to get them into a building!

your rival catering company? That sucks, and those X number of hours spent creating the best presentation are definitely Red Zone territory. The Red Zone will leave you exhausted, overwhelmed, and feeling like you want to scream, cry, or both. I get it! When a client calls to say, "Thanks so much for spending hours of your life showing us properties in Brooklyn, but we've decided we want to experience cattle ranching. We're moving to Wyoming instead. We won't be buying the $12 million brownstone after all!" I WANT TO CRY. But instead I give myself CPR so I can get out of the Red Zone and back into the positive space:

- *(C) Control*

    There are things you can't control (a client's deep desire to try cattle ranching) and things you can control. You *can* control how busy you are: how many meetings you set up in a day, how many cold calls you make, how much time you spend following up with potential clients. Stay busy; create opportunities for new work. If you stay focused on the work, the work will *heal you.*

- *(P) Perspective*

    Change your perspective on problems—*expect them.* Succeeding involves risk taking; failure and disappointment are part of that combination! So what if you had to spend an hour on the phone apologizing to Mrs. Smith about her balding dog's haircut, and then thirty minutes with your staff discussing new protocols for dog haircuts—that's part of your job. There are still many minutes left! If you had $1,000 and you lost $90 would you just say, "Well fuck it! I'll just throw the rest of the money in the trash!" No, because that would be crazy! Are you going to remember this moment twenty years from now? Probably not—chances are it's not that bad. The problem was one part of a day—it's not your whole life. Bad things WILL happen to you, and with more success comes more failure. Prepare yourself every day to *expect* failure, and you won't focus on those angry minutes as much as you used to.

♦ *(R) Re-engage*

After you've placated Mrs. Smith by assuring her this will never happen again, and that you value her business so much you'll be grooming Rex free of charge for the next year, YOU DO NOT GET TO CLOSE YOUR DOOR AND PUT YOUR HEAD ON YOUR DESK AND CRY. That's not Big Money Energy; that's feeling sorry for yourself. Do you want to spend your valuable minutes crying by yourself? Resist the urge to throw a pity party and re-engage. When a deal falls through for me, I'll reach out to a new developer and introduce myself, or I'll whip out my phone and start calling my warm contacts (warm = buying curious; hot = actively looking to buy; cold = not actively looking) so I'm back out there doing my real job, which is dominating at real estate sales! Just like the stock market, if you sell when the market is down, you're guaranteed to lose money. So, you double down. You re-invest. You take advantage of the loss and you make it up by going even harder.

Minute Killer #3:
Work Overload

I was sitting at my desk on a Sunday afternoon, watching hundreds of emails pop up. It's like my inbox had become a weed-infested garden . . . there was so much growth, it was hard to see the flowers. There were emails about offers I'd need to answer immediately, emails from potential clients, emails from sellers who had questions, emails about filming *MDLNY*, emails from developers, emails from lawyers, emails from past clients, emails from team members, emails from my Sell It Like Serhant course members, and a lot of spam. SO MANY EMAILS. Email communication is really important to my success. My clients live all over the world, but email allows us to do business efficiently. Though I get a lot of emails, I must be careful at all times not to miss anything. I carefully organize them into folders so I can easily access information about a client or deal when I need it, or when I'm scheduled to do some follow-up. Here's the thing about me AGAIN: I follow up until I die, and I spend time doing this every week. I used to block out follow-up time in my calendar, but it eventually became an automatic habit. I follow up regularly AND RELENTLESSLY.

TRIVIA TIME! According to both Microsoft and Apple, who holds the record for having the MOST EMAIL FOLDERS IN OUTLOOK?

1. Tim Cook
2. Taylor Swift
3. Ryan Serhant

The correct answer is 3! It's me! But when both Microsoft and Apple support confirmed to me that I indeed had more email folders than anyone else ON THE PLANET, I had to wonder, was this the best use of my minutes? Was I using them wisely? I decided I needed to do a time audit to see where my minutes were actually going. So, I spent a few days auditing my time in fifteen-minute intervals. Every fifteen minutes I jotted down what I was doing— whether I was on the phone, eating, brushing my teeth, or in a meeting. I did this for three days so I could get a good picture of where my minutes were actually being spent. The time I spent doing this audit was worth it to me—if spending time NOW saves me time LATER, I've come out on top in my investment.

I discovered right away that there were a few tasks I needed to take control of. I was spending ten hours a week organizing emails and eight hours a week dealing with bookkeeping. I had no idea I was spending 1,080 minutes on just email organization and bookkeeping! Crazy! In the moment, it never felt like I was spending *that* much of my precious time on those tasks, but when you add it up, I was spending one full day of minutes each week on those two tasks. Bookkeeping and organizing my emails were not a wise use of my minutes—I wanted to use those minutes to meet more clients, sell more apartments, and generate more income.

I hired a bookkeeper who would work with my accountant directly, and I hired Jasper, a.k.a. the Master of Email, to organize my email. The bookkeeper took all of the Excel work around commissions and income off my plate. I'm very anal when it comes to my money, tracking it and making sure I get paid on time for everything I do, and I always liked being in control of my own bookkeeping. But now I have a system where the bookkeeper does all the legwork, and then every week sends me an email with a full break-down that I can quickly review and approve in under 15 minutes! That savings of 480 minutes per week was a 320% return on my time, compared to what I had been spending previously by doing all the work on my own! Jasper, my email guru, worked out a system with me where I would archive every email that I didn't need in my inbox anymore, and he would go into the archive at night and sort them all by client, deal, or trade into specific folders. That way my inbox could just be full of urgent and timely emails, and then I could go to my folders for everything else. This also helped me with my follow-up and organization. I pay Jasper to do this, and he's worth every penny.

I realized I was making the mistake of thinking my time wasn't costing me anything, so I would prefer to spend minutes rather than dollars on those two tasks. But when I did my time audit, I saw that spending a few thousand dollars every month on a bookkeeper and Jasper was worth the 1,080 minutes I was saving! Time = Money. That's business 101!

When you start to think of your minutes as money, you become very careful with how you spend them. Start with a Time Audit: write down what you do every 15 minutes for a couple of days. The results may surprise you. Are you spending 100 minutes on YouTube watching puppies snuggle with babies? Are you spending 300 minutes a week doing laundry? These are your precious minutes, and you need to decide if that's where you want to spend them. Also, are there places where you aren't spending

A QUICK MASTER CLASS IN
EMAIL MANAGEMENT

I use Outlook. I find it's best for business and easier to organize than Gmail or any other email client (I've tried them all). My secret to effective email management in order to create more business and opportunities for myself? Create FOLDERS, FOLDERS, AND FOLDERS (or Tags if you like Gmail).

I organize my folders into several categories:

- Active Deals
- Active Pitches
- Admin Tasks
- Answer When Free
- Current Bills
- Important
- Urgent
- @SaneLater (This is every cold email that comes from someone I don't know.)
- @SaneNoReplies (This is every email I send that someone doesn't respond to.)

These emails sit in my main inbox and sync to all of my devices, because I need to be able to access the emails in any of these folders at any time.

On my computer, I have a folder for literally every possible thing. Every client, every listing, every trade, every year, every event, and so on. The time it takes Jasper to sort the emails saves me time, and money, in the long run. Remember, I work for Future Ryan, and he doesn't have the time to search for an email.

I do the same thing with photos: all of my photos are organized by folders per topic or event. That way I don't have to think of WHEN I took the photo, ever. I just think, I want to see that photo we took of the launch party in the Village because it might be good for the Big Money Energy newsletter. I go to the folder in three seconds and boom—minutes saved.

any minutes, but you should be? If you're only spending 20 minutes a week seeking out new business, you need to readjust your time budget. Think about how to organize your tasks so they're making your business money. Remember the FKD system from *Sell It Like Serhant*!? Mini-recap! Every day you should devote time to Finder work (that's the CEO who "finds" money for the company), Keeper work (the CFO work who runs the gamut from creating budgets to making financial projections), and Doer work (that's *the grind*—the paperwork, the phone calls, and emails). Early in your career you'll spend most of your time in Doer mode, but as you climb up the ladder you'll enter longer periods of Finder and Keeper work while you hire someone else to DO the WORK.

————

If you want to take your career up several notches and really become a millionaire in the near future, you need to step into **Task Triage**. This is a system for dividing your tasks into three different categories based on urgency, so that you don't get overwhelmed with everything you need to do every day.

Category One: Spend Your Minutes Here NOW

For me, Category One includes phone calls and correspondence from top clients or developers I want to work with. I will spend my minutes on Category One first, because this is where my minutes can turn into large commission checks and new business. Look at your audit to identify the tasks that should take priority. This is where you should be spending most of your minutes, because new business always gives you the potential to earn more money.

Category Two: Spend Zero Minutes Here

Category Two consists of tasks that are sucking your minutes dry. To be clear when I say "spend zero minutes here," that does not include TASKS YOU HATE AND THAT YOU JUST DON'T WANT TO DO. EVERY SINGLE JOB HAS TASKS THAT AREN'T PLEASANT, BUT THAT DOESN'T NECESSARILY MEAN YOU CAN PASS ALL OF THEM OFF. I don't sit down with a pile of contracts and think, Wow, this will be thrilling!, but reading them is an important part of my job, and I need to spend some minutes here whether I want to or not. Zero Minute tasks are the ones that can absolutely, 100% be done by someone else. Also, I know you may feel reluctant to let go of tasks you enjoy, or think will be hard to outsource. It wasn't easy for me to let go of my email—would another person be able to figure out how I wanted them organized? The answer was YES, another person was capable of handling this simple and straightforward task once I took the TIME to show them how. And I can now dedicate those 600 minutes to Category One tasks, which actually make me more money. Sure, outsourcing my bookkeeping and emails created overhead—but the $2,500 a month I spend on these tasks is earned back exponentially. I can make much more money with those 1,080 minutes I just bought myself, and the additional income I WILL make will pay for the new overhead in dividends.

Category Three: Spend Your Bonus Minutes Later

If I'm on a phone call that ends ten minutes early, I've just been given ten BONUS MINUTES to get even more done! To me that feels like someone just knocked on my window while I'm driving down 42nd Street, and instead of asking ME for money, he hands me ten bucks! It's like being given a present from the time gods, so I use those minutes wisely!

I keep a list handy of tasks I'd like to accomplish when surprise bonus minutes present themselves, so that I don't waste them on reading the news or checking social media. Those bonus tasks might include calling clients to see how they like their new apartment (important public relations work) or sketching out ideas for the next vlog (important branding work). If traffic was lighter than I expected, I can sit in the car before a meeting and use those bonus minutes wisely too—those bonus minutes can add up to large blocks of time where you can be working hard and increasing your income! Your competition is probably going for coffee and a donut during their bonus minutes, so grab on to them and come out ahead!

I used to wish for more hours in the day (I've been told it's simply not possible), so instead of fretting about how there is never enough time, I decided to take control of every minute. On your quest for success, remember that you are the CEO of your own bank of time. Your 1,000 minutes are yours to use however you want: you can use them to further yourself or conquer goals. You are rich with time, as rich as literally everyone else on the planet, and that time renews itself Every. Single. Day—so spend your time wisely, get things done, and you will find yourself getting closer to the amazing Big You.

CHAPTER 8

WHAT TO RISK

Robert's penthouse was amazing. It was beautifully renovated and the views of Manhattan and Central Park were incredible. I'd seen hundreds of homes in New York City, but there was something a little bit different about this one—I wanted to touch everything in the apartment. The crazy-long kitchen counter was so smooth and so shiny I wanted to hop on top of it to see if I could slide across it. The walls were covered in suede; I wanted to pet them. The open shelving held beautiful, colorful, and super-shiny objects that just screamed, *Pick me up! I know you want to!* When I dared to reach out a single finger to feel the most elegant-looking bowl that made the lemons it was holding look like a work of art, Robert said, "Yeah, we're not going to do that." Oh, sorry! Like I was a four-year-old, Robert gestured for me to sit down on his tasteful and expensive-looking modern sectional. "Oh, I can actually sit down? It's okay?" He nodded and I sat down carefully, like the sofa was made of glass and could shatter if I put all my weight on it. I looked around the room and noticed that every object in it—the artwork, vases, books, and furniture—was arranged with precision. This guy was kind of intense. I wondered if Robert was in the military. Oh my God, maybe he's an assassin.

"Ryan, I called you because I know you got a great deal on Penthouse A." I had recently sold the penthouse across the hall for $7.75 million. "I want you to get me $8 million." Before I could explain that while Robert's apartment was spectacular, and that Penthouse A had seven windows with direct views of Central Park (that's where the money is) and he only had one window with the park view, he launched into a monologue about the renovations he'd done and all of the amenities and accoutrements he'd added, like a back-lit wet bar and a high-end kitchen with ostrich-hair door pulls. I listened intently—this was all good information. But when you want to sell an apartment on Central Park, only one thing matters when it comes to price—how much frontage on the park do you have? He wouldn't be able to sell for more than the last sale I did that had more windows on the park, no matter how expensive his dandelion chandelier was (and OMG was it expensive—do you have any idea what it takes to get tiny lightbulbs inside real dandelions without the flower blowing away? and then wrapping it all in a gold metal casing? and then SHIPPING IT?). We were headed towards the usual battle about asking price.

DON'T MIRROR YOUR CLIENT'S EMOTIONS

The alarm bells were already ringing in my head. While Robert was going on at length about the artistry of his bathroom tile that had been created from pulverized volcanic rock popular with migrating miniature penguins, I knew that as soon as he stopped talking he was expecting me to mirror his passion about the apartment (IT WAS AWESOME) and also his certainty that it could demand such a high price (IT COULDN'T, even if the walls were diamond encrusted).

I learned the hard way early in my career that agreeing with a client in order to get the job can easily backfire, and it's the quickest way to getting fired. Guess what happens if you don't get what THEY decided THEY deserve? It's all your fault, and why didn't you just tell them they were asking too much! Isn't that your job? If you knew it would only sell for $2.6 million and not $3.2 million, why didn't you say something? Sometimes, in sales, I feel like a doctor who is being blamed for telling his client he has lung cancer. "You should have told me sooner! I'm suing you!"

"I . . . just met you. You . . . also shouldn't have smoked for fifty years. Just sayin'!"

You can't mirror what a client wants back to him; that often leads to a deal exploding (and your money being burned up along with it). When a client looks at you, they shouldn't see your face agreeing with Every. Single. Emotion. that they're feeling if you know they're wrong. Think about it! If you're sitting in the chair explaining to your stylist that you want a Justin Bieber–meets–Bob Marley haircut, do you want her to stand in front of the mirror with a plastic smile on her face and start chopping off your hair if she knows (thanks to her years of experience) that you're going to end up looking like a troll? Or do you want her to give you a dose of reality? "I agree it would be great to make a fun change to your style, but I'd love to talk about some other cuts that I know will flatter your face beautifully! Trust me. You'll thank me later!" If you want to be successful, you need to confidently guide clients to reality, and that's not always easy. When I need to convince people to see my point of view, I use the following tactics:

Be a Team Player

When you want to guide a client away from a bad decision, whether it's overpricing an apartment, moving forward with a disastrous haircut, or buying a pet snake for their newborn niece, they need to see you're on their side. Announcing, "What is wrong with you? Only a moron would buy a snake for a baby!" puts you and them on opposite sides. Instead you say, "Never thought of giving a snake to a baby. Could be fun? But let's think about it. What kind of snake is it? Do you have a tank for it too so little Aphrodite can watch Slithering Sam grow up safely?"

> Keep your gut reactions on the inside until you've done the math.

> Your Opinion VS. Their Opinion = Disaster.

> But Your Opinion + Their Opinion = Winning.

It's not a battle; it's a collaboration, a conversation. No matter how much you disagree with someone—if you want something they have, always show you're on their side to start. It's the only way you'll get them to trust you, and listen to you enough, so that you can guide them to a choice that results in the most positive outcome for them, but most importantly, YOU.

Be Patient but Persistent

No one ever wants to hear that the course of action they want to take isn't in their best interest. Ask my team members Yolanda, Jen, or Natalie, my three right hands—they'll tell you that when I have my mind set on something, if they just shoot it down right away it just makes my idea sound even better to me! So, they've learned to be patient but persistent with educating me on how my idea to fly a blimp over New York City to sell one of my buildings isn't . . . the most practical (although it would be fucking amazing).

Don't expect that your client will immediately abandon the idea of the haircut she's convinced will make her look like a Kardashian. It's your job to convey that what they want isn't best for them by first listening to their concerns, and then by showing empathy. Understand what they're saying, but persist in showing them the right path and provide an example of what could happen if their course of action is taken. *"I could sell you this large snake for your new niece, but if one were to present an infant to a boa constrictor, I'd have to send my invoice to the jail you'd be housed at."*

Focus on the Win

If you want a client or employer to follow your advice, create a positive picture of the End Result. "This haircut will show off your beautiful eyes, and your eyes are killer!" "This is a teddy bear, it will not eat a baby, buy this instead—she'll love it and YOU." If the goal is to sell, then your win is to collect a commission. Everything in the middle is just noise, and like the professional adult you are, you don't yell back at loud noise, you don't put your hands over your ears and yell, "YADA YADA YADA I CAN'T HEAR YOU!" and you don't put on noise-canceling headphones, either, to block it all out. You listen to the noise, and you absorb the best and leave the rest.

I calmly explained to Robert, after listening to him for forty-five minutes, that his finishes were gorgeous. I honestly loved them and had never seen such detail before in screws. But, based on the comparable sales I had, $7 million was the right asking price given his upgrades—if he hadn't done such an AMAZING renovation, we would be talking about a price closer to $6 million. At $7 million I believed the apartment would sell quickly (taking up less of Robert's time), and the return on his initial investment would still be massive. We would get to his End Result.

CODE #12

Always focus on a client's goal to get to YOUR win.

TRYING ISN'T GOOD ENOUGH

To Robert's credit, he heard me out and agreed on my valuation. He was keen to make a return on his investment quickly (and apparently without humans messing up his perfect apartment). He wanted to leave room for negotiation though, so we settled on a listing price of $7.895 million.

"But, Ryan, there's one thing." My smile started to fade. "Ryan, I don't want people coming in here and touching my stuff." Wow, could he tell just by looking at me that I wanted to take a nap on his pillow walls? They looked so plush!

"So, there will be no parties, no open houses, and no physical showings without first making an offer."

No open houses and no showings? Whoa. While many clients are understandably worried about having people in their homes, this was next level. I have shown thousands of apartments, and never once have I taken someone through the kitchen only to have them peek into the fridge and say, "Oh great, there's lasagna. I'm just going to heat up a plate of this real quick. Want some?" What was his real concern? And how was I going to sell his penthouse if I couldn't actually . . . show it? Robert went on with his lecture like I was a kid about to be left home alone for the first time.

"Seriously, no one—not a single person comes in here unless they are very well vetted and have made an offer." While I understood his concerns—this was his home, not mine, after all—I wondered exactly how I'd get people interested enough to make an offer if they were not actually allowed to set foot inside the apartment? People don't generally drop $7 million on a property they aren't allowed to enter. And we weren't exactly experiencing the joy that is a seller's market.

"Well, normally I have a photographer come in and take pictures so that I can get people interested. Then I host a brokers' open house with the top agents in New York to build up excitement." Robert looked at me like I had three heads. "No. No open houses. But if you want to come in here and take a few pictures with your little camera, I guess that's okay." My heart was sinking again; I had just secured this great penthouse listing, but had no way to show it to anyone. The End Result was drifting away from us fast.

"How about a video? Look at these views! People need to be able to see how great this place is." Robert sat back in his perfectly designed chair made of sharp right angles. "Okay. Sure. A quick video. Make sure you get the view." We shook hands, and I left the apartment feeling an equal mix of excitement and frustration. This was a huge listing, but how could I get the word out about this great property if humans weren't allowed on the premises? I wanted to sell it, I wanted to earn the commission, but this was a challenge I had never faced before. I had made tough sales — wonky layouts, complete lack of light, no view — but in those cases I worked hard to find a positive (who needs a view if you work late at night? Weird layout . . . no, it's an *interesting* layout!), but I was allowed to bring clients INTO THE APARTMENT. I was going to have to dig deep and get really creative if I wanted to see a commission check on this one.

Later that night, I met my friend Nick at a bar in the East Village. He was friends with the lead singer in the band that was performing. I stood in the crowd with my drink, feeling conspicuous. I was the only guy there in a suit, and my good shoes were sticking to the beer that was spilled all over the floor. Was I the only person left in the city who didn't have full-sleeve tattoos? The band was great and everyone was having fun dancing. After the set, Nick dragged me through a dingy hallway that smelled like pee. Shortly after getting my head stuck in a cobweb, we reached a door at the end of the hall where the band was hanging out in a tiny room before going back onstage. Nick introduced me to Mary and the other members of her group. When Nick asked, "So, did you guys ever find a cool space to shoot your music video?" the wheels in my brain started spinning. The lead singer shook her head no. *Wait a minute.* Robert said I could make a video! What if instead of a quiet and boring little listing video like every other broker makes, I make a music video—in the apartment! My mouth was faster than my brain. "I have the perfect place for you! It's a super-cool apartment—a penthouse overlooking Central Park." Everyone's eyes lit up: a penthouse? They needed a free great space, I needed a great listing video. But it would all have to be done on the sly, because I was pretty sure that if Robert found out about it, he would murder me in my sleep. This would either go down as one of the worst or best ideas of my life.

I started making plans for the video like I was planning a jewel heist. This was a luxury residential skyscraper just off Central Park. You basically can't bring a pencil into a building like this without getting insurance and permission and sign-offs from like, nine people. So, I obviously couldn't drag an entire band through the lobby of this fancy doorman building and up the elevator to the apartment with no questions asked. Surely Robert had spies planted throughout the building who would rat on me, even if he had already given me permission to enter his apartment? I could just imagine the kind of chat that could happen in the elevator: "Oh, hi, Robert. I meant to tell you. The other day I saw your broker, the really tall, gray-haired guy, and about fifteen suspicious characters (they looked like musicians!) bringing a huge drum set, a bunch of camera equipment, a few guitars, a saxophone, and a tambourine into your apartment. Okay! Have a great day." And then my life would be over.

I needed to get someone on our side, someone who could aid in the mission. Late one night, I headed uptown to Robert's building. I introduced myself to the late-night doorman. I explained that I needed to make a listing video so I could sell Penthouse B, but I needed to do it (1) in the middle of the night and (2) without getting caught so I'd (3) need access to the service elevator without the owner knowing. I made sure to add that the video was a "surprise" for Robert, and that everyone would be lip-syncing and pretending to play their instruments. No sleep would be harmed during the making of the music video! The doorman agreed to let us in the following night—well, morning. We would start shooting at 1 A.M. and bust out of there by 5 A.M. It would be like we were never even there!

The night/morning of the shoot I was a nervous wreck. Was I doing the right thing? I believed with every fiber of my being that I could sell this apartment—but not unless I could actually show people how great it was with a unique video. I took a deep breath as we rode up in the service elevator: I can do this. I was going to make this work.

CODE #13

Once a decision is made, never waiver.
All energy is directed towards ensuring its success.

My anxiety flew through the roof of Robert's perfect penthouse as the director started setting up cameras and lights. I looked around for security cameras or a nanny cam but couldn't find one, but that didn't mean Robert hadn't hidden a *Mission Impossible* camera in the walls somewhere! Ugh. There was equipment everywhere. Because I had acting experience, it was decided that I would play a role in the video. Would this video serve as documentation of my very last moments on earth? Would this be all my parents had left of me? I pictured my mom watching the video in Colorado, crying into a tissue. "Where did we go wrong?" Every time I heard a noise, I was convinced it was the FBI, sent in by Robert to break up our covert op. While the director was working hard to make a cool and artsy music video, I was whisper-shouting out instructions like: "Did you get a shot of the bathroom? People need to see the tub!" And: "Make sure the shot includes the entire kitchen! We need to show all of the appliances!" This might have been a music video, but I had an apartment to sell and I needed this to come out as the most creative real estate listing video ever made. After what felt like the longest night ever, the band left, the camera equipment was taken out, and I spent the next few hours inspecting every square inch of Robert's apartment. I had to eliminate the evidence. I left at 7 A.M. and headed home to change and get ready for the day on no sleep.

When Robert announced that there was "one thing," and that thing turned out to be a huge hindrance to my selling his apartment, I had two choices: Say NO—because selling a $7 million apartment that no one can see is impossible. Or

... move forward, tapping into some Jedi-master Yoda wisdom: *"Do or do not do. There is no try."* When I made that decision to make a music video I CHOSE TO DO. Trying wasn't enough in this situation. Trying would have been having a few photographs to show potential clients, and that's not enough to close a deal. That's not DOING. That scenario would have left me beaten down by anger and frustration, because I would have let the seller's restrictions prevent me from doing my job. I would have spent weeks not selling his apartment, being mad at Robert, letting the entire situation suck—and for what? To ultimately admit defeat after wasting my time and everyone else's time? To cry about it to Emilia every night while eating Cinnamon Toast Crunch? That is not the path of BME. Instead, I chose to DO. I had to make lemonade out of the lemon I had to work with. And it was a pretty shitty lemon—like a moldy one that had rolled under Robert's gold refrigerator months ago.

The video did its job and, thank the sales gods, it showcased the apartment beautifully and caught the eye of both brokers and buyers. Most just thought it was crazy that I would do a full-on music video in a high-end penthouse, but the fact that they actually watched it, and made those comments, meant I had succeeded. I had captured everyone's attention, and that's my job as a sales and business person.

Most importantly, I had captured the attention of a woman named Cora who saw the video on YouTube and really liked it. Cora's father, who she affectionately called "Faja," was willing to spend many millions of dollars for a nice place for his princess.

You know who else saw that video? Robert did, and when he called me I felt like I was going to be grounded.

"RYAN SERHANT?! An acquaintance just sent me a very interesting music video. Is that my apartment? Because it sure looks like my apartment!"

Before I could answer and explain it had done the job and we had a great offer, Robert shouted, "Ryan I know it's MY apartment because YOU are in the video! You're rolling around in MY 4,000-thread-count Egyptian cottons!"*

When Robert finally stopped shouting, I told him about the offer. He went silent for a full minute. Then he spoke: "That's too low. Can you get them up?" While I knew Robert hadn't forgiven me about the music video that quickly, it's amazing what presenting someone with $6.5 million in cash will do to their mood. The bottom line was we had an offer to work with, and he'd be making a huge return on his investment. My Yoda-inspired DOING had resulted in a potential sale in record time, and we wanted to get this deal done. I did what I needed to do (create a way for people to see inside of the apartment), I took a huge RISK, and I was making a huge commission as a result. Knowing when to forge ahead with a risk and when to hold back is one of the key things that separates small earners from huge earners.

I suspect the offer lessened the pain of the video (even if someone did flush the toilet, which was another of Robert's rules that I broke). After some back-and-forth with Cora's faja, a deal was reached for $7 million, exactly where I told Robert it would sell in the first place. Robert was happy with his deal and I got to live. Hooray!

---

*I wasn't actually rolling around. I was casually lying on my side trying to look cool because it was a music video.

RISK ASSESSMENT: SHOULD YOU GO THERE?

The anxiety I felt during the filming process was next level, and I vowed I would never do something that crazy—EVER AGAIN. But when no one was harmed in the making of the video and I made the sale, the risk seemed well worth it (and I think the seller would actually, but very reluctantly, agree!). Pushing the envelope is required if you want to make millions, but it can be hard to know if you're about to go too far. Now, when I have a crazy idea (when don't I have a crazy idea?) I run through the following questions before moving forward:

What is the worst-case scenario? Be serious; really think about it. I knew I could get fired for making the video, but I wasn't doing anything ILLEGAL! Getting fired from this job would have been bad, but it wouldn't have derailed my entire career.

Look at the situation from all angles. Could you lose lots of clients, your reputation, all of your money? Be honest about the worst thing that can happen before you move forward, and be ready to accept those consequences.

What is the plan, and can you execute it? I didn't just randomly decide "Oh, a music video would be cool!" and then spend tons of my time, which could have been used selling other things, to produce a damn music video. I had a band already lined up, I had access to a director, and he was able to get the equipment required to pull this off. You have to stretch to make money, but don't be unreasonable about what you can actually accomplish.

Is there another option? If I could have thought of a better way to show the apartment (and had the ability to pull it off), whether it was drones, robots, specially trained dogs (dogs aren't people! he never said anything about dogs!), I would have happily abandoned the ridiculous plan to make a video. Before moving forward with a wild idea, make sure there isn't something else you can do that is simpler and less risky! Pulling off wild stunts (not that I know anything about that) isn't easy, and sometimes it involves laying out money (do you have any idea how much it costs to rent a DeLorean should you decide to throw an '80s party to sell an outdated apartment?—*a lot*). Don't do crazy for the sake of doing crazy—remember that the end goal of taking this risk should be to increase your income.

Can you anticipate obstacles in advance? There were a lot of obstacles when it came to making that music video; a neighbor could tattle on us, my client could walk in and find me *in his bed* that I was using to shoot a scene (unlikely because I knew he was out of town), a guitar could scratch one of his perfect walls. My list went on and on. However, I was confident that these were obstacles I could handle. The band came in in the dark of night, no instruments were actually played . . . they pretended! No noise! And I set ground rules for everyone about how careful we had to be. Taking a risk is smarter and more likely to result in success (and your wallet getting fatter) if you take the time to run through the what-ifs. Know what can go wrong and PLAN, PLAN, AND PLAN.

While the saga of the music video ended happily, I was also prepared to deal with the outcome if it didn't. DOING doesn't always end the way you want it to. I decided to take the risk and that means I was ultimately responsible for whatever happened, which could have meant losing a client, losing a deal, or even being banned from the entire building! Bringing a band into the apartment was a huge risk, but it was worth it to me if it meant creating the tool I needed to get my job done. Do or don't do!!

And, if it went the other way? If Robert fired me and I lost out on a huge commission? That would have sucked, but I wouldn't have pointed fingers at anyone but myself. I wouldn't have been angry with Robert about firing me or making my job hard (I accepted it under his terms and I could have walked away). I wouldn't have played the "if only" game—*if only I hadn't snuck a band in!* In the end, making millions isn't about being perfect—it's not about never making mistakes. It's about making the absolute best out of what you've got. It's about DOING. And the next time a moldy lemon is tossed my way? I'm going to do the same thing—I'll stay positive, think creatively, and do what I think is right. If I end up with a perfect glass of lemonade, then awesome! If I don't, well that's on me but I won't stop trying to make something amazing.

BIG MONEY ENERGY

MANTRA #2

Earning millions of dollars starts with a simple but powerful belief—that there's no limit to how much money you can actually make. There's not! Sometimes, the biggest obstacles between you and a massive paycheck are the negative thoughts that have set up camp in your brain. Kick those thoughts out forever by reminding yourself that you CAN MAKE MILLIONS.

I AM BRILLIANT

I AM POLISHED

I AM DESERVING

I HAVE BIG MONEY ENERGY

THE BLUEPRINT: EARN MORE

Money is essential to staying alive, but we've all been trained not to talk about it because it's *private*. It creates ego, contempt, jealousy, anger! What someone makes is, we're told, what they're worth as humans, so IT'S NOT POLITE TO TALK ABOUT MONEY! While money is the entrée to a better lifestyle, earning more also provides freedom, security, access, and puts you in a much better position to practice generosity. There is nothing wrong with wanting more money, and the phrase about money being the root of all evil is false. It's not like you instantly turn into a greedy monster the second your bank account has seven figures in it! Obviously, there are a lot of problems that can't be solved with money, but a higher income equals *more options*. And don't you want the freedom to live the way you want to?

Avoid Bullshit Money Energy

Seen + Heard + Remembered

- **Acknowledge people.** Something as simple as a compliment on their shoes works EVERY SINGLE TIME.
- **Ask a question.** The question should be something that allows you to learn something about the other person. It could be anything from if they live in the neighborhood or where they work, to if they like dogs.
- **Commit an interesting fact to memory.** Be curious; focus on what's different about the person you are talking to, and remember it so you can refer to that fact later.

When you step in a pile of bullshit

- Get the deal done as quickly as possible—and GET OUT.

The best course of action is to get yourself away from the bullshitter as quickly as possible so you can *cash that check.*

- **Establish boundaries.** Tell the bullshitter what is acceptable, and let them know what actions you are taking. If they know how hard you're working on their behalf they'll be more likely to stay within the boundaries you've established.
- **Want to know where you fall on the BME/BULLSHIT meter?** Go to www.bigmoneyenergy.com/quiz/

Dress like you dominate

- **Dress for the right audience.** Who exactly do you need to influence or impress? What are the expectations?
- **Wear a "security blanket" if it boosts your confidence.** A fake Rolex for me might be a fake LV bag for you. Whatever works!
- **Practice FIT, CLEAN, SHINED.** Your clothes should fit you impeccably and be perfectly cared for, and your shoes should shine like the star you are.
- **Have a confidence costume.** While you're creating your look, have at least one outfit that makes you feel like a million bucks every time you put it on.

Kill highly contagious problems or DIE

- **Recognize the Signs:** reluctance, reaction, and retraction. If someone doesn't want to let go, is having insane reactions to normal requests, and is threatening to kill a deal over nonsense, you have to TAKE CONTROL OR YOU WILL LOSE YOUR DEAL.

- **Utilize the Three Cs:** calm, control, and conviction. Calm responses are powerful—do not get upset! Take control of the situation by establishing your "no-go zone," the one area where *no way are you budging*. Speak firmly—do not waver! Wavering is like wearing a T-shirt that says, I DON'T MEAN ANYTHING I'M SAYING SO CONTINUE TO WALK ALL OVER ME.
- **Keep some cards close to your chest:** Some details are best left unshared.
- **MAP it out:** Is it material information that must be disclosed? Do you have an answer to the problem so you can solve it quickly? What is the client's personality? This is about trust—do they want to know everything? Or, do they count on you to make problems vanish without them being bothered?

The 1,000-minute rule

- **Know your minute killers.** Be self-aware about where your time gets wasted.
  - #1 *The Perfection Trap.* TAG yourself out: Trust you know what you're doing. Ask for help from someone who excels in this area. Give yourself a reasonable time limit and honor it!
  - #2 *The Red Zone.* Those ugly situations when something has gone wrong and has the power to derail your day or even your week. To fix this, give yourself CPR: You can't Control everything; stay focused on what you can control. Perspective—change it. Expect problems as part of a successful career so you don't *freak out*

every time something goes wrong. Re-engage. Get back out there and do your job! Take an action, any action, to get back in the game!

#3 *Task Overload.* Manage your emails. Perform task triage. Audit your time; what are you really doing all day long? Determine where to spend your valuable minutes, what tasks you should outsource, and what to do with those glorious bonus minutes.

Don't mirror your client's emotions

- **Never be defensive.** Always see their side. You are a team!

- **Be patient but persistent.** No one wants to hear their ideas aren't great. Persist in showing them the right path, and provide examples of what could happen if their course of action is followed.

- **Focus on the Win.** Show them the positives that will result from following your advice.

- **Assess your risk.** What's the worst-case scenario if you take a big risk? Be honest with yourself! What is the plan? Can you reasonably execute this? Is there another option? If there is, take it! Don't do crazy for the sake of crazy. Be crazy with purpose! Anticipate obstacles in advance so you are prepared to handle them. Your goal is to have NO surprises!

ENERGY

There's something extraordinary about you, and people know it. It's clear that you're powerful, but it's balanced out by your warmth and friendliness, and everyone around you wants to soak up some of your light. You are fascinating yet approachable, fiercely intelligent but easy to talk to. Your energy is so bright and infectious that people are lining up to meet you. You are the picture of Big Money Energy.

CHAPTER 9

EVOLVE OR DIE

As 2019 was coming to a close, I knew I was one of the most fortunate human beings on the entire planet. My amazing wife, Emilia, and I had expanded from a pair to a trio—our daughter, Zena, was almost a year old and already sharing her opinions on real estate by babbling loudly every time I took a call with a client. The renovations on our family townhouse in Brooklyn were moving along slowly but surely, and the Serhant Team had dominated the rankings, selling nearly a billion dollars a year for three years in a row (if you add in what we put into contract, we did nearly $1.5 billion in transactions in 2019 alone!). If that weren't enough, I wrote my first book, *Sell It Like Serhant,* and the vlog and online sales course were exploding with success. The membership course had added nearly 4,000 students in over seventy countries in less than five months. I was killing it! And then *hello*, nice to meet you, brand new decade! As we ushered in 2020, I wanted to shout, "I'm king of the world" from the terrace of my penthouse like I was Leonardo DiCaprio in *Titanic*. I had it all—and I was SO GRATEFUL. As I reflected on how not too long ago I didn't have enough money in the bank to buy groceries, I had to wonder, Is this it for me? Life is great but what is next? Should I just stop and be happy with everything I already have? Should I just settle and be okay with being okay?

As I shivered on my terrace channeling my inner LDC, it occurred to me that after his dramatic proclamation on the hull of that ship, things started to go really, really, wrong. We all know what happened. The luxury liner was believed to be such a marvel of engineering that IT WAS UNSINK-ABLE. Nothing can take this ship down—it is impenetrable! Wait, did we just hit an iceberg? *Oh, shit.* The *Titanic* started sinking slowly, and about two and a half hours later she plunged to her death in the icy waters of the north Atlantic Ocean (tragically taking 1,500 souls). As I looked around, the lights of New York City sparkling like icicles, I thought . . . Wow, I could go down too. NOTHING IS UNSINKABLE. If I didn't change course, I was going to become compla-cent. What could I do to stay on top of my game?

Change is a constant when it comes to achieving success in anything. If you commit to an exercise plan, dutifully working out every day, you *will* see positive results. People will notice: "Wow, you look awesome." You've made great progress—your favorite jeans fit! You feel so good you want to take it even further, so you keep going to the gym, do-ing the same workout that has gotten you this far. But huh, that magic seems to be gone. What's up? What's up is that change is the spice of life and without it life tastes bland. Lots of people will tell you change is unnecessary, or "Don't try to fix something that isn't broken"—I think that is total bullshit. IF YOU AREN'T EVOLVING, YOU ARE DYING OUT. If you think you can just sit back and go with the flow because you've achieved a certain level of success, you're going to sink eventually. Whether you are CEO of a profitable business that you started, or top dog at a corporate company, you have to stay one step ahead of everyone else.

In 2019, I ended the decade on top of the world as the top broker in New York City working for *someone else*. It was time to change, anticipate, modify, or up my game if I didn't want to start sinking. No way was I going to let everything I had worked for fizzle out and die. I'd have to look beyond my current success to see what was out on the horizon. What would I find if I kept pushing forward and exploring?

After much contemplation/fretting/planning and exciting discussions with my team about what was possible (so much!), I decided to launch SERHANT. It wasn't easy—leaving the brokerage where I had worked my entire career felt like getting a divorce, and there were so many legal issues to sort out and terms to negotiate.

SERHANT. is the most followed real estate brand in the world, calibrated for the marketplace of tomorrow, delivering proven results for buyers, sellers, and developers. SERHANT. revolutionizes the traditional brokerage model by innovating through media and content creation, and is powered by a full-service, in-house film studio as well as an amplification platform that puts our properties in front of more people than anyone else.*

While I was excited to build a brand new business of my own, it also meant kissing my first-place status goodbye. Starting over meant I would now officially be in last place.

---

*After months of think tank–style discussions and countless arguments, this is what we managed to come up with.

That was a hard pill to swallow, but it meant there was nowhere to go but up. But apparently I could go down even further than I imagined.

THE $72 MILLION DAY FROM HELL

Prep for the new business was heavily under way with BIG plans, and I was still selling a significant amount of real estate while transitioning from my previous brokerage to my very own company. It was all happening, and it was such an adrenaline rush! And . . . spring 2020, Covid-19 shuts down the world, and then the entire city. People are getting sick and dying, and the economy is tanking. The stock market sells off 10,000 points seemingly overnight. Restaurants, bars, stores, gyms, hair salons, and offices have all shut down. The city that never sleeps is eerily silent. The panicked calls from clients were coming in constantly:

"Hi, Ryan, we've decided not to move forward with buying the brownstone on the Upper West Side—it's not the right time for us to upgrade given what's going on."

"Ryan, New York is DEAD, I'm pulling my contract."

"Ryan, my family and I decided to move to Montana and buy a rare-buffalo farm because that seems like the rational choice for us now. Sorry, but we won't be signing that $20 million contract you negotiated for us for six months."

The real estate market in New York City had been decimated due to Covid-19. I'm not going to lie—I was terrified. I had just taken the biggest financial risk of my life when I decided to start my own company (which no one knew, by the way). I was about to have a huge payroll to cover and massive other expenses. Everyone was gripped by fear and not buying; how would I survive? I actually considered backing out and going back to my old employer and just staying put. *It's not the right time.* Surely everyone would agree that it's a ridiculous time to start a new company. It wouldn't matter if I waited another year before I took the plunge.

I worried constantly about what the right course of action was. I lost so much sleep. Each phone call and email from another stressed-out client weighed on me; the pressure was so heavy it was tempting to lie down and let it crush me. When I was with my previous brokerage, they covered all of the overhead (rent, expenses, payroll, marketing, everything!) in exchange for a percentage of my commission. I was responsible for the livelihood of my team, and it was scary.

I felt like I was down for the count, and it was the worst feeling ever. When I thought about putting the new company on hold, I didn't feel any better—I craved the independence, the newness, the possibilities. I didn't want to give up on myself. But how could I find the energy to wade through this huge mess?

It's not like I hadn't had to pick myself up before.

———

In August of 2019, I experienced what I now refer to as "Hell Monday." If Hell Monday were a movie, there would be scenes of me going to the gym and getting ready for work with ominous music playing, and dark lighting to clearly indicate SOMETHING AWFUL IS GOING TO HAPPEN TO THAT GUY.

New York real estate is intrinsically tied to the rises, and brutal falls, of the stock market. Whether or not a buyer is financially affected by a crashing stock market, the simple fear when the market goes into the red is enough to make any buyer in New York panic and pull out of a transaction. New Yorkers have thick skin, but no one has forgotten the financial crisis, and everyone is convinced the next one is always right around the corner. That Monday in August, the Dow Jones Industrial Average began to plummet on fears that China would retaliate against the US, given Trump's recent tariff threats. By lunchtime, the market had sold off 950 points. I had been fielding calls all day from clients, doing my best to reassure them:

"The stock market goes up and down, and we are so far up from 2016. This little blip shouldn't deter you from the home you're about to buy to raise a family in for years and years."

Whatever I said didn't matter. I still got calls like this:

"Hi, Ryan, so my buyer has decided not to take the penthouse in Chelsea."

"Why?"

"He's decided to pursue a different path."

What does that even mean? You can't live on a path! Damn, another buyer drops out due to fear.

I was riffling through my bag of ideas, trying to save the deal, when my phone rang again . . . with equally bad news about a brownstone in Brooklyn. Hell Monday was relentless—it was like one punch in the face after another. Deals were falling through, people were backing out, and none of my usual rescue tactics were working. By the end of Hell Monday we had lost eleven deals, totaling . . .

$72 MILLION!!!

That's a lot of deals, right? There are always deals that fall apart, but I had never lost that many in one week, much less a day! It was crazy and IT SUCKED SO BAD. I had never faced so much loss all at once. What if this was just the beginning? If things got worse, what would happen to me and my family? What would happen to my team? Would I have to use my sales skills to sell snake oil on the street? Was the anxiety I was feeling actually the start of a massive coronary. . . . oh my God, am I going to drop dead in my office? I'm too young! The flood of feelings I faced that day were overwhelming—they hurt.

But there's something you need to know about the moment you lose a huge deal, get fired, face a massive disappointment, or have a FULL-ON HELL DAY. It's not just a shitty day; it's also the moment when the people who win are separated out from everyone else. And which camp do you want to be in? Camp Win or Camp Lose?

As I sat surrounded by the carnage of dead deals at the end of Hell Monday, I knew I didn't want this mess to be my legacy. I was number one at the beginning of the day. I didn't work this hard to watch it all go down the drain. Part of me just wanted to put my head down on my desk and cry (maybe I did, for a little while). But I couldn't spend the rest of my life hiding in my office; I had to find the strength to tap into my energy reserves and keep going.

I got out my calendar and put a big, fat, red circle around the date that fell four weeks after Hell Monday. I jotted down the feelings I was having: despair, fear, anger, frustration, desperation. I also wrote down "$72 million"—to remind myself of *the horror*. Life and work went on. While I was obviously worried about the loss of commission on that

THE POSITIVE/NEGATIVE CHALLENGE
An Exercise

When it comes to a day in the life of someone with Big Money Energy—POSITIVE ALWAYS WINS. You have to train yourself to gravitate towards the positive, high-five yourself for the small wins, and let the negative shit fade into the background. Back when my family used to call me Cryin' Ryan (yes, because I cried constantly), I could find the dark spot in any situation. Disneyland? So hot! Long lines! Mickey Mouse is weird! Christmas? It's only twenty-four hours and I'm asleep for like a third of it! You can't solve the injustices of the world, but you can stop living in a dark cloud of your own making.

There's an easy way to break this habit. Take a piece of paper and fold it down the middle. As you move through your day, write the good things down on the positive side and the negative things down on the other. If your oatmeal tasted good at breakfast . . . write that down! Every time you notice something positive, add it to the list. Keep doing the challenge until your positive side is much longer than the negative! On the massive mindfuck that was Hell Monday, my positive/negative exercise would have looked like this:

Positive
- Lifted heavier weights at the gym before work!
- Got to work without being run over by a taxi.
- I'm actually alive.
- I have a family and friends.
- There is food in my refrigerator.
- My team is hardworking and awesome.

Negative
- Had the worst day of my life at work EVER.
- I'm overwhelmed and scared for what's next.
- I lost sooooooooooo much money.

huge number, I had to accept that I couldn't get it back. I had to forge ahead to make new deals and take on new listings. I was determined to survive this blow.

Four weeks later, I saw that red circle. It had been a month since the worst day of my career. Did the anger and all of those other gross feelings vanish immediately? No, they did not. But was I a walking and talking ball of rage a month later? Not as much. I was alive, I was still standing, and that meant I could survive. Big Money Energy is about rising above, searching for the light in the darkest and gloomiest of places. When I marked that date on my calendar, I was training my brain to seek out the positive energy. It's always there to be found, but sometimes (especially after a loss) you have to take a little more time and look a little bit harder—but it's ALWAYS there. I do this after every major loss, and my mind doesn't get as easily stressed or angered by the things I cannot control. Other people's decisions don't upset me as much. I know that with time I will heal, so I live in the moment and no longer waste a single minute of my life on dread or fear. DREAD IS DEAD TO ME.

When you're facing a big career loss of any kind, it's not the time to sit idly and wait for things to magically improve. During this pandemic, LOTS of people have told me to "sit tight," hang on, and wait for the New York City market to come back. *No, thank you.* I might have been knocked on my ass, but I wasn't going to stay sprawled out on the sidewalk while everyone else stepped over my crumpled body. I was going to double down. I was going to speed up without losing control. I didn't really know what was on the other side, but I wasn't going to wait for everyone to pass me by.

While everyone else was cutting back, remaining calm, and waiting it out—I was going to go harder. I'd hire more team members, more admin, get a new office space, rethink my approach, and rework my business plan. When you're faced with a loss—take an action, *any action*. Ask yourself what you can do right now to plan your own comeback. Take INITIATIVE. Initiative is your life raft.

YOU HAVE CONTROL

When I started my new company, I had fantasies of making a huge splash with our first sale. I imagined selling a $30 million penthouse on billionaires' row on our first day—something that would catch everyone's attention. The headlines in my mind read: RYAN AND HIS NEW COMPANY DOMINATE! Instead, my first client was a nice . . . rental. I thought my rental days were long gone, but I was in uncharted waters with the shutdown and I wasn't in a position to be picky.

Asha and Arjun were from San Francisco, but they had a passion for showing their daughters *the world,* and wanted to spend a year living in New York City. They wanted a three- or four-bedroom apartment and had a budget of $10,000 a month. I showed them several great options, and they were having trouble choosing. I decided to show them one more apartment in Tribeca that I knew they would love. It was a great location, it had fantastic views, and it had a large outdoor space, which I knew was very important to them. "We like to be close to the stars" Asha had said. I could tell they loved the apartment as soon as we walked in. "Wow, how much is the rent for this one, Ryan?" Asha was smiling from ear to ear; I suspected she was picking out furniture in her mind. "Actually, this one is $12.5 million. It's not a rental." Before Asha and Arjun could speak, I told them that with interest rates being soooooo low, it was actually cheaper in the long run to buy than rent.

We started with a low-ball offer of $6 million, because who wouldn't want an apartment at 55% off? After more back-and-forth than a tennis match, we got to $8 million flat, and the developer would credit them a $1 million in closing costs and furniture. Asha and Arjun now owned their own little part of Manhattan, close to the stars, for a significant discount. I was so thrilled to have turned my renters into buyers that I put on a star-spangled suit to celebrate their closing.

CODE #14

Starting over isn't starting from scratch;
you still have your skills and experience.
It's not starting over—it's starting again.

I only made this sale because after the entire city shut down, I forced myself to take *one small step*. I didn't want to revisit rentals at that stage in my career, but I just needed to keep moving. Taking on that rental led me to an unexpected sale. That sale gave me the energy I needed to keep going, and while business hasn't necessarily recovered, I'm confident I can survive because I'm 1000% prepared for whatever will hit me in the face next.

I don't know what the next week, month, or even year will bring—but I'm prepared to be flexible, to evolve and adapt, so I can make it through whatever craziness comes next: alien invasion, zombies, land sharks, you name it. No matter what happens, remember that *you have control*. You can stand up and take one small step at any time. It doesn't have to be big! You don't have to wait for someone to tell you it's safe, or it's a good idea! You have the power to take a single step. You have the power to create the change you want.

CHAPTER 10

BEING SELF-MADE

Wood for Sale $50 a Cord

Jack Ryan Wood

Ask for Ryan or Jack

617-456-7890

I started my first business when I was ten, and I thought my plan was *genius*. At the time, my family was living on a farm outside of Boston. There was a forest surrounding our house that hadn't been touched since the '60s, and my dad was having many of the trees taken down to make room for a yard, a driveway, and some walking paths. One day I was at the grocery store with my mother, begging her to buy Jell-O pudding cups, when a sign caught my eye:

WOOD FOR SALE

Wait. People actually pay for wood? I was picturing the never-ending rows of trees in our yard—every one of them now represented cold, hard cash! I had been living on a gold mine this whole time and I had no idea! If my dad was just going to give the chopped-down trees away, I could sell the wood as firewood instead, and make enough money to buy the video camera I wanted (video cameras were very expensive in the mid-'90s)! As soon as we got home, I found my younger brother Jack, who was seven. My older brother had already moved out, so it was just us two. "Hey, so I have a business idea. Let's start a wood business." Jack's eyes lit up. "All we have to do is cut up the trees that are lying all over the place and sell it as firewood! And we'll call the business Jack Ryan Wood! We'll make tons of money. It is going to be AWESOME." Jack was down (he didn't really have a choice), and from that moment on we spent every spare second we weren't in school chopping up trees with a dangerous gas-powered wood splitter. We pooled our meager cash supplies that we had saved from our allowances and discovered we had $13.75. My father kindly agreed to lend us a few more dollars so we could place an ad for Jack Ryan Wood in the Topsfield, Massachusetts, newspaper. A few days later my mom yelled to me while I was outside operating a potentially limb-severing power tool: "Ryan! There's someone on the phone for you. He says he actually wants to buy firewood!" I couldn't have been more excited if Superman himself was calling. "Hello? This is Ryan of Jack Ryan Wood." *Wow, I'm on a business call!*

"I want two cords. Can you deliver it? I need it delivered tomorrow by five!" said the voice of our very first customer.

My ten-year-old mind almost exploded. I was about to make $100! "Deliver it? Oh, sure!" I jotted down the address and hung up the phone. WOW, MY FIRST SALE AND I NAILED IT! I AM GOING TO BE SO RICH FROM SELLING ALL THESE TREES TO COLD BOSTONIANS!

I walked into the living room where my parents were reading and announced we had made our first sale. My dad briefly glanced up from his newspaper. "That's nice, Ryan. Good job."

"I sold two cords and I said we'd deliver it, so can you drive us?" I asked. My parents looked at me like I had just asked for twelve puppies. And that's when my mother delivered one of the harshest business lessons I have ever learned. "NO. It's your business, Ryan, so it's your problem. If you want to be in business for yourself, you have to figure things out . . . for . . . yourself." *Oh, okay. I'm ten.*

It was a fairly big problem, as it was clear that my brother's toy wagon could not accommodate such a large order. While I was standing there wishing I could snap my fingers and transform myself into a licensed driver, I heard a noise coming from the other side of the yard. It was Biff, the guy my dad hired to do some basic repairs and odd jobs around the house. Biff drove a very large, bright-red pickup truck. *Wait a minute.* Maybe I could cut a deal! "Hi, um, Biff? So, my brother and I started a business selling firewood. We made our first sale! Can you drive us to deliver it? I'll cut you in." Biff shrugged, put down the extra-sharp ax he was wielding and said, "Yeah, sure. I'll drive you." Now, we had sold two cords. To those of you reading who have no idea what a cord is, it's a stack of firewood that roughly measures out to eight feet long by four feet high and four feet wide and weighs—wait for it—about 5,000 pounds. I hadn't really thought this through when I made the ad to sell wood, or when I agreed very quickly over the phone to deliver it! Jack and I spent what felt like an eternity loading up the pickup with as much wood as we could, which ended up being only about half a cord. Ugh. We would have to make four trips, and I definitely didn't tell Biff that. Jack and I hopped in the front seat and we were off. About ten minutes later, we arrived at the top of a very long, winding country driveway. An older man, a.k.a. *our first customer ever,* waved at us. "Can you please drive it down to my porch?" He shouted.

I replied, "Sure!"

I was already thinking about my video camera that I'd be able to buy if we kept making deals like this. Suddenly, I noticed that Biff looked kind of angry. "Hey, kid. This was not part of the deal. No way, bud."

I remembered my mother's advice to always ask for things politely. "Can we *please* just drive the wood to his porch? It's not far!" I didn't dare even tell him we would have to do this . . . three more times.

How had I not noticed how scary looking Biff was until just this second? "Listen, kid. This is America and I don't have to do anything I don't want to do." With that proclamation, he got out of the pickup truck, flipped a lever that raised the bed, and dumped 2,500 pounds of wood right onto the ground with a deafening roar. Wood was blocking the entrance to the driveway, logs were rolling out onto the road in every direction. It looked like a forest had just exploded. Biff ordered us out of his vehicle, then backed out of the old man's driveway, drove over a log, and peeled off. I froze. The old man just looked at the mess and said, "Well. That's not what I'm paying for. I'll pay you when that wood is stacked up on my porch. And that doesn't look like two cords either. I know my wood."

I couldn't believe what was happening. This transaction had been going so well and was going to kick-start my newfound wood wealth. Now it was going terribly, and I had no idea how to fix the situation. I wanted to follow through on the deal I made with our customer, but I also wanted to cry. How was I supposed to carry all this wood with my seven-year-old brother who I FORCED into this job? How was I supposed to tell this guy I had no way of getting the remaining wood to him? I wanted my mom. *Sales is brutal and I hadn't even made a full sale yet!* If only my ten-year-old self knew then how much crazier it would be in the future when I swapped firewood for multimillion-dollar apartments.

Now I was cold and stranded on the side of Route 128 with half a cord of wood and my seven-year-old brother. What do I do? Do we just leave and forget this ever happened? That seemed mean—the old man would have to pick up all the wood himself (what if he died while doing it? would that make me a murderer? what if he called the police and we were arrested for being the worst wood sales boys ever?). And I was also determined to get the full payment, so I would be closer to having enough for my video camera.

I decided I needed to seek counsel from my dad, and to do that I needed to walk home. I looked at my tiny, shivering brother. No way was he up for the walk, so I shoved him in a bush (sorry, Jack). I walked the two miles home, cursing myself the entire time. What was I thinking? Why did I promise delivery when I didn't have that system in place yet? How could I have subcontracted out such an important job to Biff? He turned out to be completely unreliable! I dreaded telling my parents that I was falling flat on my face during my very first business venture. *Why is the world such a cold, dark place? I always hated that red truck!* I finally made it home, and I fessed up to my dad about what had happened and said I needed help to finish the job and get paid. Part of me hoped I'd be wrapped in a blanket, shoved in front of the TV, and given a steaming cup of cocoa. "What a terrible ordeal you've been through, son! Let me make it better." But that's not what happened. My dad was furious. Forget the wood—I had left little Jack in a bush on the side of a highway because I was too focused on making money and didn't care about anything, or anyone, else. He got his coat. "We are going to get your brother, but you have to finish your job. You wanted this business. You made a commitment. You need to follow through, or you'll never learn."

When we arrived back at the old man's house, the wood seemed never ending. The next six hours were the longest of my short life. It was freezing cold, my arms ached, and at one point during the long, painful process I sat down exhausted. I was close to crying—again. My dad helped me back up. "Ryan, I know this is hard, but this is the commitment you made. That means that no matter how you feel about it, you're sticking to your promise until the very end. Otherwise, your customers will never trust you about anything, and you won't have a business. But don't forget there's a big reward waiting for you when you finish the work. Do you want all of this hard work to be for nothing?" At that moment, kind of. All I could think about was going home! I finished the first half-cord, told the customer I was sorry for the bad experience, and let him know that I wouldn't be able to bring the remaining wood to his house because I didn't have a way to deliver it. He looked at me like he was looking at a dying baby deer. "That's half a cord?" Yes. "Okay. Well, here's $25 for what you brought me today. And here's another $25 for the rest of it if you tell me where it is. I can have someone get it tomorrow. I remember my first business too. Deal?" My eyes lit up. For one, I now had FIFTY WHOLE DOLLARS. I thought about being angry for a second because it wasn't the full hundred, but then I realized it was better than zero because I wasn't fulfilling my end of the transaction. Deal.

WHEN YOU HIT THE CROSSROADS

In every single venture of your life—whether it's starting a new business or job, writing a book, losing weight, or training for an Iron Man, you will find yourself at *the Crossroads*. The Crossroads are located at the intersection of WINNING and LOSING. You'll know you're there because you will feel like shit. All that fresh enthusiasm? GONE. And that deep sense of purpose that you had not long ago? BULLSHIT. It abandoned you with a pile of problems, and now you're sitting in a puddle of self-doubt. IT'S GROSS. The worst thing about the Crossroads is that it can break you. You can feel so crushed that you'll give up—even though your big success could be right around the corner!

When you find yourself in this dark, scary place you can commit to staying on the road for winners, knowing you'll have to tap into your energy to navigate the tricky terrain as it comes and eventually . . . someday, you'll get what you want. Or, you can give up. You can crawl along the loser road that's littered with regret, where you'll rest in a grave-yard of crushed souls and broken dreams with headstones that say: IF ONLY I HAD TRIED HARDER. *Is there anything more horrifying?*

CODE #15

Successful people make decisions based on
their commitments. Amateurs make decisions
based on how they feel.

Life is full of crossroads! Now when I hit one, I know how massive the repercussions can be. It's tempting to give up—let your clients and colleagues down, ruin your reputation, trash your finances, and ignore every commitment you made. But what about that commitment you made to yourself? To follow a dream and achieve massive success? You get one life—you either use your resources, act on your great ideas, and make good use of your time, or you don't. You can't get any of those back!

Even when I was ten, I didn't want my hard work to be for nothing. I thought about Biff (so mean!), the hours of cutting and loading wood, the long walk home, abandoning my brother under a shrub—did I want to give up? Did I want to feel like a failure at ten? Or did I want my video camera? The answer was clear. We made the deal with the customer for him to get the rest of the wood we had already cut up, I got paid half of what I thought I would make from the deal, and I quit sales the very next day for the rest of my life.* I was a kid, so obviously the stakes were much

---

*In this case, the rest of my life was until September 15, 2008.

lower, but when you prioritize commitments you made over how you feel, you have a formula to rise above nearly any-thing—you become unstoppable.

OUTLAST EVERYONE

When my mom declined the role of delivery driver in my first business venture, I learned that if I wanted to succeed I'd have to be self-made. And when Biff sped off and left us alone on the side of the road, I learned I didn't want to have to depend on anyone else for my success ever again. My mom didn't have to drop the newspaper she was read-ing just because her son wanted something and wasn't old enough to drive. It isn't anyone's job to make your dreams come true or solve your problems. No one owes you any-thing just because you have a great idea, work hard, or are incredibly talented. To succeed and earn millions, you must have the wherewithal to surge ahead when all you want to do is lie down with cake and ice cream and give up. And there isn't going to be a team of spectators cheering for you to get off your ass and keep running down the winning road either. A lot of people can sell one big thing, write one best-selling book, or make one awesome touchdown. And that's great! But if you don't want to be a one-hit wonder, if you want to experience one big success after another, you need the energy to *keep* running!

I KNOW it's not easy. I can be juggling three deals, talking to the accountant about payroll for my new company, help-ing one of my agents with a negotiation, recording the Big Money Energy podcast, planning shoots for the vlog and

Million Dollar Listing, and meeting with Pro members in my Sell It Like Serhant sales course, all while trying to get home to see Zena before she goes to sleep, when suddenly my email stops working and I'm like . . . Really?! *Can I just walk out the door and go straight home so I can hide under a blanket? Why does nothing work, ever?!* I probably could just go home and call it quits for the day, but that's acting on *how I feel*, which is what toddlers do. Honoring my commitments (even if I want to lie down and cry) is what successful, high-achieving adults do. That's the difference between amateurs and professionals. If you're making all of your decisions based on how you feel, know that you have a long way to go. Once you're following through on your decisions, then you're well on your way to being a pro. I have made a commitment to myself and my company to succeed, so I created a system to make it easier for you to follow the path you've committed to taking.

Structure

Think of being surrounded by imaginary walls made out of fierce discipline, incredible focus, and impenetrable systems. This is the massive superstructure you create to house and protect your success. Take a minute to look at it. How strong are the walls around your success standing? When it's time to work, do you get to it? Or does it take you forever to get to work because you spend twenty minutes digging through old pizza boxes with orange Cheeto fingers before you unbury your laptop? Be honest. If you're going out four or five times a week drinking bourbon flights with your homies, oversleeping in the morning so that you don't make it to the gym and are scrambling to get to work, you are operating under a flawed structure that will eventually collapse.

My structure stands strong because I go to the gym every morning (even if I'd rather be sleeping), I always bring healthy food with me and stay within my eating window so I'm not grabbing desperation pizza for lunch every day, and I carefully schedule my time in fifteen-minute increments for the entire day, Sunday through Friday. Some calls may be booked for one fifteen-minute block because I know they'll be short, while some meetings might require six blocks of time. And even when I don't want to do the work, I still do it because I've made that commitment to the client, the people who work for me, and the man in the mirror.

Before I go to bed, I review what I'm going to be doing the next day so I feel prepared. That's the structure *I need* to keep me going when the path gets rocky.

Think about what *you need*. Remove distractions if you can, do not open your social media accounts, and tell your friends you are unavailable to text until 5 P.M. If having a messy desk distracts you, make sure you spend ten minutes cleaning it at the end of the day so you are setting yourself up for success the next day. Have a list of goals printed out to inspire you to keep at it—and if you're planning to reward yourself with that handbag you've had your eye on if you finish a project—print out a picture of it and tape it up where you can see it! I want you to get that handbag! Add "deep work mode" in your schedule and insist that you not be interrupted during that block of time unless there is a disaster of massive proportions—flood, fire, or Godzilla attack. Babies have strict schedules: when they eat, when they nap, when they do tummy time. We grow

up and think that just because we can make our own decisions, we don't need the same structure. But we DO—to
survive and to GROW.

Plan

This is your very own road map to success: it's your *how*.
You might be grinding away every single day of your life,
but you need a plan to ensure you're moving forward with
purpose. How exactly are you going to get to where you
want to be? Think about resources and tools you need to
reach your goal. Connect with people who can help you
get there—that could mean hiring an assistant or just outsourcing all of your laundry. Make the investment to get
your time BACK!

Create actionable steps and keep track of your progress.
But here is the thing about plans. Sometimes the universe
looks at your plan and lets out a deep belly laugh. You could
be moving along, making progress and enjoying some real
successes when *hello, the bridge has been washed out, so
what are you going to do?* Will you jump? Crawl down the
hill and hop over the water? Go a different direction? Build
a new bridge? Changing course as needed puts you in a
position to succeed when others might stand on the ledge
thinking all is lost. All is not lost! Using a different tactic
does not mean you failed; it means you're being *smart*.

My original plan when I came to New York City was to
be a great actor. When that didn't work out and I ran out
of money, my plan changed but my desire for success did
not. I decided I wanted to be great at renting apartments,
but it was clear that the terrain was very limited. I could do
the same thing over and over and enjoy a limited amount of

success—or I could adjust my plan and start selling apartments, which would take me where I wanted to go faster. Selling brought me so much further down the road that I wanted to prepare to explore even more. Now part of my plan is to expand into a new area every single year.

When creating your own plan, let yourself think about how far you can go, determine what tools and resources you need, and be prepared to shift course when a big pile of mess is dropped right at your feet.

Outlast

You've created a healthy structure for yourself, you've made a plan—you've changed that plan as needed . . . so can I have the success right now please? No, you can't. People who make millions of dollars know that doing everything right doesn't mean success arrives on your doorstep wrapped up in a pretty bow NEXT TUESDAY. So, when is it coming? Next month, next year? In a decade?! Maybe, maybe, and yeah, maybe. Success is a *long game*. That means putting in the work and staying committed even though there's no clear view of the success that's waiting for you. Outlasting everyone else is about stamina, tenacity, and getting comfortable with the unknown.

You can never really know what will be required of you to keep the commitment you made to yourself to succeed. Last week I had an apartment to show. It was a magnificent three-bedroom on the Upper East Side with four terraces and views of Central Park. This legit Master of the Universe apartment has an asking price of $14 million. It was 100 degrees outside, I was sweating buckets in my suit, and when I walked into the kitchen I blurted, *"Oh shit."* Right there, on the expensive marble counter, was a gang of cockroaches.* You know what can ruin an unobstructed view of Central Park on a picture-perfect New York City summer day for a very rich buyer? COCKROACHES RUNNING AMOK IN A KITCHEN! My client was minutes away, so I just crushed those little monsters. I didn't cry, I didn't scream, I didn't call the super—I took care of the problem myself immediately. Why? Because (a) I am 100% committed to my success and (b) the moment I think *any part* of this job is beneath me is the same moment I start to lose ground. To be clear, I have many people to help me and I would never have reached this level of success without my team. But when Yuriy goes on vacation, I'm not going to throw my hands in the air and cancel all my appointments and spend the week watching Netflix. I'll mask up, glove up, and take the subway wherever I need to go. If no one on my team is available to take photographs of an apartment and it needs to be done . . . I'll do it.

Outlasting your competition is about maintaining momentum on the road to success. It's about *getting stuff done* no matter what. It takes total commitment if you want to reach the pinnacle of success—even if that means crushing hard-shelled bugs with your bare hands. It isn't anyone else's job *but mine* to carry me to the success that I want in my life. What about you—are you totally committed to your goals and ready to dominate? What is stopping you from making the commitment to your vision?

---

*I know what you're thinking. How does a $14 million apartment have roaches? It's New York and unfortunately they are everywhere. Roaches love expensive real estate too!

The moment when Biff the angry trucker blocked an entire road with all that wood, I was ironically set on the path to success. I was literally at a crossroads (Route 128 and the old guy's driveway) and I had a choice to make. Do I find a way to stick it out and finish the job I set out to do? Or do I turn my back on the giant mess I'm responsible for and just move on with my young life of cartoons and snack foods? Life tosses big and small obstacles in our paths whenever life feels like it—we can't control that, but we can control how we choose to respond. Are you going to push through and use all of the resources at your disposal to forge ahead—or are you going to sit down on the side of that cold, lonely road all by yourself and give up? You will want to at times, but what are you doing this for? Yourself—success, your dream of writing a book, starting a company, or buying a house? WHATEVER IT IS YOU WANT IS STILL YOURS FOR THE TAKING, but only if you keep moving forward. It might be for just a few minutes—or the walk could take hours, days, weeks, months, or years—but when you reach that spot in the road where your success is waiting for you, it will all be worth it. When I held that shiny new video camera, by doing a lot more chores and finally getting the money together, and made my first-ever movie called *The Nair Witch Project*—about a bunch of witches in our woods who would try to take our newly grown leg hair because it made us MEN—it was like Biff, the deadly power tools, the old man, and the giant mess of wood wasn't really so bad after all. It was just an obstacle on my first-ever road to success and I knew when faced with another crazy situation, on another road, that I'd be able to handle that one too.

CHAPTER 11

BUILD YOUR
ROUND TABLE

There are few things I won't do to sell an apartment, other than commit a felony or harm animals. That's because my reputation for going above and beyond to get a deal done is key to my success. I've shown apartments in the middle of the night (more than once), I've thrown insane parties, and I once built a craft room to convince a little old lady that, yes, this apartment is perfect for your bow-making passion! If you want to rise to the top of your field, you need to constantly ask yourself, *"What else can I do?"* What kind of crazy giveaways, parties, or antics can you use to cement yourself as the number-one person in your field in the minds of your customers? I WILL DO NEARLY ANYTHING.

Recently, I found myself in a situation where it seemed like I might have gone too far. It started after I sold an $11 million apartment on West 67th Street to a college kid named Weng, who had a very wealthy and very generous father back in Shanghai. A few months later, Weng called me from the virtual reality room of his insane new apartment to tell me that his dad, Wing, wanted to buy an apartment in New York City for himself. YES! After Weng and I showed Wing lots of apartments over FaceTime, he decided on a spectacular apartment on the thirty-fourth floor of a new building on Park Avenue. The asking price? $40 million. *HELL YES*. I worked my magic and negotiated it down to $36 million. Wing just needed to sign the contract and pay the deposit!

Cue minor problem that has the potential to grow into a big problem and unravel it all. Because interest rates are so cheap, Wing decides he wants to get a loan. That's fine, but it will take time to put together, and other people wanted the apartment badly enough to pay all cash. To complicate the situation, due to the demands of being a textile tycoon, Wing *is now missing*. But Weng is certain his dad wants the apartment! And because of the deal I did for Weng, I know Wing is good for it!

The other broker was breathing down my neck for the deposit—and there was no way I was letting go of a $36 million sale due to a mysterious textile emergency. I called my banker, wired $1.8 million of my own money, and signed the contract myself.

The second I put the pen down I thought, Oh my God—now it's actually me who is in contract for a $36 million apartment. What was I thinking?

Wing is not returning my calls. Wing is not answering emails. I'm becoming increasingly nervous. I felt like I sneezed at an auction and accidentally bought a Picasso. I didn't want to damage my reputation. I didn't want to have to call up the other broker and say, *"Oops, it was actually me who bought the apartment, but I can't really afford it . . .*

soooooo sorry." I also knew Wing really wanted the apartment, and I didn't want to lose it to another buyer!

I decide there's one thing left to do. I bought plane tickets to Shanghai for myself, Weng, and Scott (the best mortgage broker in the world, who was helping me out with this insane transaction). We managed to nail down an appointment with Wing and his business manager, Tony Chow, to sign the papers and retrieve my $1.8 million. Relief . . . almost.

After the longest flight in the world, we are picked up by Tony Chow. Our meeting with Wing was the next day, so we had some time to kill that night, even though all I wanted was to June Shen myself to sleep. Tony drives through the city like a maniac, awkwardly barking off landmarks, giving me flashbacks to my *MDLNY* audition. We make a quick stop at the fake market . . . fake iPhones, fake handbags, fake everything, where I buy a cool Ferrari phone for myself. I want to go to our hotel and pass out, but Tony has other ideas. He abruptly pulls over and parks his BMW on *the sidewalk* in front of a night club . . . "Okay! Let's have fun now!" The nightclub is insane—Tony is throwing back scotch and introducing everyone to his "American friends." It's nearly 3 A.M. and I'm blurry from exhaustion, and where the fuck is Scott? I can't find Scott! At that moment Tony pulls on my sleeve, let's go now! Wait, should Tony be driving? Before I could ascertain what Tony's blood alcohol level could be, I'm shoved in the front seat and Tony is flying through the city . . . red lights? Why bother stopping for those? Eventually, we end up at Tony's house—on a golf course that appears to be on an island, somewhere in the gigantic city that I have never been to before on the other side of the WORLD. WHERE AM I?

Tony immediately passes out. I have no idea where I am, and I don't know where Scott is. *Is Scott alive?* My phone is dead, I can't find any landlines. I briefly consider stealing Tony's car, but I know I won't be able to read the street signs. I feel genuinely fucked—like I'm in some twisted, dark sequel of the *Hangover* movie franchise. Am I going to run into Mike Tyson and a tiger if I try to find the bathroom? Our meeting with Wing is happening in two hours. Tony might not need to be there, but I sure as hell had to make that meeting, and I was so tired I couldn't feel my face. I flew across the planet to see this guy, get a signed contract, and get my money back! Suddenly I hear something.

MY FERRARI PHONE IS RINGING.

Thank you, faux market! I am greatly relieved to hear Scott's voice on the other end. He's alive and at the hotel! Scott does his best to explain to the front-desk person at the hotel that his friend has BEEN KIDNAPPED, and they kindly help me figure out how to get a taxi from Tony's house so I can get back to the hotel, change, and get to the meeting with Wing. Tony was still passed out in his bathtub, clutching a half-eaten ice cream sandwich, when the taxi arrived. I manage to catch a few minutes of sleep in the car. When I got to the hotel, I slapped myself in the face five times, cleaned up, and told Scott I'd explain where I had been later. Somehow, we manage to get to Wing's office on time. The door opens, and standing there as fresh as a fucking daisy is Tony Chow. What the literal McFuck-stick is going on?! Less than two hours ago this guy was bathtub soup. But Tony, who has made a miraculous full recovery, has the papers and the check ready to go. "Mr. Wing appreciates your dedication to life and would like to proceed with this glorious transaction." Aha, great. As soon as I had the contracts and the check for the $1.8 million in my hand, I could put Tony Chow and his partying behind me. I had gone WAY above and beyond . . . and while terrifying, it had been worth it. I had saved a $36 million deal. I slept like a baby the entire flight home, knowing I didn't have to call the other broker and explain we were backing out of the deal. My reputation for getting impossible deals done was firmly intact!

MOVE BEYOND MEDIOCRE

That was the only time I ever got kidnapped (kind of) in the name of a deal, and the first time I ever used my own money to secure an apartment. DOES ANYTHING SAY "ABOVE AND BEYOND" MORE THAN PAYING A SEVEN-FIGURE DOWN PAYMENT, SIGNING A CONTRACT, AND FLYING TO FUCKING CHINA TO BE KIDNAPPED BY THE BUYER'S BUSINESS MANAGER? I don't think so! While this was obviously a more dramatic example of what I'll do, I know that without my reputation as the "above and beyond broker," I sink back into a sea of nameless, faceless real estate brokers. I'm just a regular guy, and that's not good enough.

Your reputation is one of your most powerful forms of currency. If you think you can succeed without knowing what people say about you when you're not in the room, *you're wrong*. Your reputation is the sum total of all the energy you put out into the world. Whether it's being the smartest and most efficient guy to work with—everyone loves working with you! Or, maybe you're known for being innovative and solving problems in a unique way, and people seek you out for this reason. Your reputation is your brand.

If you want the world to view you as a fierce competitor, a killer businessperson, and overall Dominator there are some key qualities you must have, and they need to be in balance.

To create this powerful combination, think about it like you were gathering guests at a dinner party: you want the right mixture of people with different interests and backgrounds to keep the evening flowing. To succeed on the highest of levels . . . your "table" needs to consist of a good reputation, healthy competition, a tiny dose of revenge to fuel you when you're low, a strong ability to focus, and a way to manage life's tasks so they don't derail you from your real goal . . . which is to make millions of dollars. Each of these qualities is equally important—one cannot overshadow the other, or your energy will be off. If this happens, you could come off as an ultra-competitive jerk or a revenge-driven maniac. *That's not good energy.*

The idea of a round table isn't new (it's actually very, very old). Legend has it (I'm a theater nerd; I like a good legend!) that King Arthur and his knights gathered at a massive round table somewhere in his mystical castle.* It was round on purpose. Everyone was equal, everyone's ideas mattered—a knight couldn't waltz in and say, "Man,

---

*I wonder, what is the cost per square foot for a mystical castle?

I am by far the most chivalrous motherfucker here. SO, I DESERVE TO SIT AT THE HEAD OF THE TABLE. Move over, Arthur!" Not even the king held a special position above the rest of the knights. At a round table, competition can't take over everything else . . . ruining the balance and pulling you down.

When I started selling real estate in 2008, I didn't have a team, but that didn't mean I was doing it totally alone; I had my round table to help provide guidance and tough love. Whether you're a team of one or you work at a company of thousands, you need to create your very own *virtual round table* for guidance and inspiration.

Reputation

You do not have to fly to China to have a good reputation. But you do need to know how you are perceived in your community. If it's "nice kid"—like pre-BME Ryan—you need to think about what steps you can take to show the world how capable you are. You might need to do more networking, or be more vocal about your wins to current and potential clients. Your reputation can grow like weeds . . . so what's being spread around needs to be *positive*. Your reputation also provides you with a bar to measure yourself against. If you are the "smartest financial advisor in town," you have to maintain that reputation!

Competition

Since the moment I started selling real estate, I've been fueled by competition. It started with Ben, the killer broker in my office who would rent an apartment every three seconds while I struggled to manage even one deal. Once I got on *MDLNY*, it was my fellow cast mate Fredrik (who I'm always compared to and forever will be). Fredrik came to the show much older than me, with a lot more experience than I had, and I fought hard to catch up. Now, I think of my competition on broader terms—the literal thousands of other brokers in New York City who are selling apartments, nipping at my heels as I write this, and the brokerage companies themselves that I now compete with since starting my own firm in the middle of a pandemic! There is no game without competition. Competition gives you an edge; it provides something to push off against. Think about it! There is no Coke without Pepsi, no Nike without Adidas, and no Microsoft without Apple. Being number one means nothing if it's *just you*. When it comes to competition, you can sit down on the sidewalk and watch the race because *ughhhh . . . competition is so exhausting*. Or, you can get swept up in the energy and let it carry you towards the finish line.

You can "compete" with anyone you want: your co-worker who has brilliant ideas and manages to execute them flawlessly, your boss who is constantly nailing pitch meetings (how does he do it every single time?!), your life-long friend who is a stellar negotiator, or someone you've never even met before. You don't need to be best friends with Kylie Jenner to be inspired by what she's achieved with her makeup business. It doesn't matter that you've never met Joe Rogan. If his success in the podcast industry makes you hustle harder, offer him a "seat at your table." Unless you are 110% satisfied with the way your life looks like RIGHT NOW (and really, are you? is this as far as you think you can go?), you need a clear vision of success to compete against. Let people who have reached a high level of success provide that picture for you! Follow them on social. Read articles they've written, write down their brilliant quotes and put them where you can see them, create a folder of images that make you think, THAT IS WHAT I WANT FROM LIFE AND I WON'T STOP UNTIL IT'S MINE. Be inspired, execute great work, and emulate their success!

When I first started out in the real estate business, I wasn't taken seriously. I didn't grow up in the city. I didn't go to fancy schools with kids who lived on Park Avenue, I didn't have any contacts, I worked at a brand new brokerage house that no one had ever heard of, and I used to get lost downtown with alarming regularity. Word would get back to me that other brokers used to say, "Ryan Serhant? That guy is a joke! He's never going anywhere." *Oh, really?* And guess what? That comment hurt. It really fucking pissed me off! I'm not proud to admit it, but underneath my expensive dress shirt you'll find a big fat chip on my shoulder about my "lack of pedigree." I'm still angry about being called a joke, but I'm careful not to let it blossom into full-fledged RAGE (rage can eat you alive, and you can't compete if there's nothing left of you). But if you hold on to just a tiny bit of that anger, you can channel it into *motivation revenge*—a relentless drive to do your best and prove that all your haters and doubters are wrong.

If I think for even half a second that Steve Ferguson should just *give me* his new project on Devoe Street because we've worked together twice (and we sold out at record numbers both times!), I immediately take an action to secure this job. I'll call, email, schedule a lunch, send a gift! Anything to remind him that I exist and I always go above and beyond for him. I can't let myself forget that other brokers are saying, "Ryan's too busy now running a company," "Ryan is just a reality TV broker, he doesn't really sell. He's a joke! Hire me!" Just thinking about being called a joke makes me want to work even harder. To be extra clear, this is not *John Wick you-stole-my-car-and-killed-my-dead-wife's-dog-so-prepare-to-die*–style revenge. Motivation revenge WILL NOT LAND YOU IN JAIL because it never involves actually hurting anyone or anything, because that would be crazy. Motivation revenge is about sprinkling a little extra magic out there to show your haters what you've known all along—that you're *awesome*.

Your Who

Weird question: Do you know why racehorses wear masks with blinders? It's not just for show. The blinders actually have an important purpose. If a racehorse looks around during a race, even for a split second, they lose speed. The blinders keep the horse 100% focused on its task—which is *winning*. Secretariat, the greatest racehorse in the world, didn't look back to see if his archrival Sham was closing in. Secretariat kept his eye on the finish line and ran like hell to get there because *winners only focus on winning*. Humans can't wear blinders, but we have to stay 100% focused on winning, as if we were. This isn't always easy to do; everyone gets slapped in the face by doubt, or knocked on their ass by fear of failure, or distracted by a competitor who might be running a little faster. This is why you need someone at your table who forces you to look straight ahead. This person is your WHO, and they'll keep you running steady even when you want to stop.

Every Sunday, after I come home from the gym but before I go to the office, Zena and I have a standing date to hang out together. She can't say much yet, but in my mind we're talking about cool things like mermaids, the original formation of the continents 750 million years ago, glitter, and how she'll conquer the world when she's older. Her hopeful smile is the perfect anecdote to any fear or doubts I'm having about starting a company from scratch during one of the most difficult times in recent American history. I could get sidetracked EASILY by the economy, the uncertainty, the enormous risk and financial pressure, but I'm not going to fail. Zena is my WHO. I will do whatever it takes to show her how much is actually possible when you aim high, work hard, and stay focused. Your WHO is the person who makes the hard work worth it; failing them is not an option. Your WHO might be your partner, child, sibling . . . or it can be YOU! That's fine! What matters is that you don't let your WHO down.

CODE #16

Every goal needs a picture of success.
Visualize what your big success looks like daily.

Task Master

You can't experience record-breaking success if you have no idea how you're going to handle all of the random life tasks that will easily suck up your minutes. As you move up the ladder, you obviously have more freedom to outsource the tasks that suck up your time and energy, but what can you move off your plate RIGHT NOW? When I was first starting to sell apartments, I found extra minutes in my week by paying for valet laundry service instead of doing it myself. The money I spent outsourcing this task paid for itself, since I was able to use the time to earn more money. Eventually, I was able to hire a junior agent to show apartments for me, so I could focus my time on building new business to bring in more dollars, instead of just handling current business.

At this point in my career, the two big tasks I have to master, to preserve my minutes so I can succeed like crazy, are food preparation and transportation. Every day, a lunch bag the size of a toddler is dropped off at my apartment. Inside of it is all of my food for the entire day. Healthy meals, two protein shakes, lean meats with lots of vegetables, and enough snacks to keep me fueled up for the day. I do not want to spend a single minute thinking about what I'm going to eat or where it's going to come from. It's done—it's all in my enormous lunch bag! Having Yuriy to navigate the madness of the city streets so I can work in the car between appointments is also *huge*. My car is my second office, and there are days when I'm in the car more than I am anywhere else. Having a driver enables me to double my output throughout the day. For me, outsourcing these tasks is *priceless*. How are you mastering your tasks so they don't drain you? If you currently have a team, is there someone who can take more off your plate so you can do your real job of making more money? If you're working solo, will it help to outsource laundry, cleaning, errands, and grocery shopping? Don't underestimate how important it is to have this kind of support as you're taking your career to the next level. Re-evaluate how you need to master your tasks so you can GET MORE DONE.

THERE ARE NO LONE MILLIONAIRES

No one succeeds all on their own. Long before I was making millions of dollars, I had important people in my life who pushed me and provided the perspective I needed to keep going. I have no idea what I'd be doing today if my older brother Jimmy hadn't told me to "Stop being such a little bitch" when I felt like quitting my job. I know I wouldn't have earned millions of dollars if Emilia didn't remind me to "cry on the inside like a winner," and I'd probably cry on television with much greater frequency. You might feel like you need to do it all, but no one succeeds without support. Every millionaire has been buoyed by a competitor, their haters, and their WHO. No millionaire would have a reputation for anything if it weren't for customers and clients, and I don't think anyone got rich doing laundry all day.

If you saw my previous office on *MDLNY*, you know that the Serhant Team worked in a fairly traditional office space: reception area, conference room, lots of desks and phones . . . a giant tub of Twizzlers for afternoon sugar cravings. Just recently, I left the brokerage firm I'd been at for the first twelve years of my career and I started my own company. I left the standard office model in the past and planned a path for the future of work. My new company works in our product, *a house*. It's homey enough to feel comfortable, but it's also classy and polished so we can impress potential clients.

As I write this book, there is one thing that's noticeably missing from the *SERHANT. House* though—*desks*. We are really owning the home vibe! Instead of desks, team members get settled in a comfy chair in the lounge with their laptops or, if it's a nice day, work outside on the roof deck. My favorite place to work in our new non-office is the massive, round table in the dining room. I love working side by side with various team members knowing together we are going to make amazing things happen.

The table in the dining room of "SERHANT. House New York" is big, and there's always a few spots open for other people, and I love the symbolism of that. THERE'S ALWAYS ROOM FOR MORE. THERE'S A SEAT OPEN FOR AWESOMENESS. Even King Arthur kept one seat at his table vacant at all times. The crazy story goes that Merlin (what legend is complete without a wizard?) was out in the world looking for the Holy Grail (as one does) and it was expected that one day he would return to the table with this magical object that brought infinite happiness and abundance . . . and *eternal youth*. Merlin is bringing eternal youth, people! So save him a seat!

I'm not holding out for a holy grail, but I love the idea of leaving a space open for sheer awesomeness. Now, when there's an empty chair at our table, I know it's not just a vacancy—it represents infinite possibility. That chair is a reminder that I should remain open to new opportunities and even bigger successes. If you want to make millions, curate your table with the people you need to crush your goals.

Compete like crazy—toss in a dash of revenge. Maintain your reputation, learn to delegate, and maintain focus—all of it is key. But don't forget to leave an open space . . . you have no idea who may come along and want to sit down.

CHAPTER 12

OPPORTUNITY IS ALWAYS KNOCKING

A couple of years into my career, I had the opportunity to interview to be the sales director of a large condo development downtown. Landing this deal would be a huge boost for my career, which was finally gaining traction. I was selling more, had gained plenty of experience, and knew I was ready to stretch—but I was still terrified to go into this interview.

I was meeting with Winston Hendricks, one of the most powerful real estate developers in New York City. Winston bought his first property in the early 1970s, in the Village. A few years later he was able to sell the building at a hefty profit. Forty years later, Winston had transformed that first brownstone into a $3 billion real estate empire by flipping properties one after the other, amassing property all over New York City. He was a titan of the real estate industry. You couldn't get a meeting with him even if you were family. Now do you see why I was nervous?

When I was brought into the conference room of his Madison Avenue office (in the Madison Avenue office BUILDING he owned), my anxiety level skyrocketed. Spread out before me, like a lake of mahogany, was the largest boardroom table I had ever seen. How did it even get in here? Was the entire building constructed around this insane table? I did a quick count—sixty chairs? What kinds of meetings go on with sixty people? I've since named these types of spaces *intimidation rooms.*

I was about to sit down but suddenly I froze. Oh my God, I didn't know which chair I should sit in. What if this is a test? If I don't choose a chair right away, will they think I'm indecisive? But choosing quickly could also be bad—he'll think I'm impulsive! But there's too many choices! What happened to regular-sized tables with normal amounts of chairs? Is he watching me through a one-way mirror right now, grading my every thought? What a mind fuck!

I had finally settled myself in the dead center of the table when Leah, the head of sales, came in. She was wearing a sharp, black suit and walked purposefully towards the very end of the table and sat down. She was a couple of dozen chairs to my left, but thankfully I could still hear her when she said, "Good morning. Sell me on why you should have our building?"

I launched into my semi-prepared speech I had memorized, laden with adjectives about my intense work ethic and dedication. Just as I finished speaking, Sofia, Winston's second in command, came in.

She sat at the other end of the table . . . we were now three people at a table for sixty, spread out literally as far as the eye could see.

"Sorry I'm late. Good morning, why should we hire you?" Shitty shit muffins. Like her colleague, Sofia exuded confidence and poise . . . and apparently hadn't thought of a different question. I quickly gave a modified version of my first speech, using different adjectives, and added that I thought I could bring a fresh and imaginative approach to the marketing aspect of the building. Whew, just as I breathed a sigh of relief, the door opened *again*.

It was like time slowed down. An incredibly polished and very tan man wearing the most expensive-looking suit I have ever seen entered the room.

His glasses were *perfect*. I wish I needed glasses! On his wrist was a large, shiny, rose-gold watch. It was so beautiful, it's like I was mesmerized by it. For a second I swore I saw his aura; it was the same shade of green as money. This exemplary Alpha sat down right across from me and said just two words:

"WHY YOU?"

NOT AGAIN!

The room was silent. I swallowed my fear, and possibly my tongue. I breathed. I can do this. For the third time I semi-improvised another version of my speech. I was dedicated and passionate, I was diligent, I had fresh ideas. Winston in all his splendor made me want this job even more! Suddenly, I heard myself speaking without thoughts that typically precede the formation of actual words: "AND I WILL BE SO COMMITTED TO SELLING OUT YOUR PROJECT THAT I WILL TATTOO THE ADDRESS OF YOUR BUILDING INTO MY CHEST."

Cue long, awkward silence. *Is the interview over?*

I saw a smirk pass over Winston's face . . . "Well, that's crazy," Leah said. "Thank you for coming, we'll get back to you."

I left the meeting feeling like a freak. Did I actually say I'd get a tattoo? On my chest?! Getting inked was not part of my plan! But I felt something else. As I sat at that massive table with people who were 100% dominating at life, I thought—Wait a minute. I was sitting there too! I wasn't the guy who dropped off the bagels; I was part of the conversation. If you had connected the dots between the four of us at that table, we would have made a diamond! Maybe I wasn't ready to sit at the head of the world's longest conference table, but I had climbed high enough that I could reach opportunities, as long as I had enough guts to try and grab them.

The word "opportunist" is often associated with negativity. *"Kevin tried to steal all your clients when you were in the hospital after a trapeze accident. Who tries to take someone's clients while they are recovering after shattering all of their toes and fingers? He's such an opportunist,"* you yell in rage! Let's be clear about something. That's not being an opportunist; that's being a dick. Anyone who would take advantage of a situation to exploit others or step on people to get ahead is a jerk. But given that you hadn't been hospitalized or hurt, Kevin didn't steal anything: you were absent and he seized the opportunity. If you want to be successful, you have to seize the opportunities that are presented to you.

Set your ego in place right now. If you want to dominate at life, understand this: *all* successful people are opportunists.

These people jump on great opportunities with zero hesitation. They think big and know they'll figure out a way to turn each opportunity into a success.

The tricky thing about opportunities is that they don't care about how busy you are or if you're "ready" for them.

It's whether or not you show up that matters most. If your dream position at work is up for grabs, or a dream client is in town, but you hesitate because you have that really big vacation planned and you're trying to finish up your workload before you tour Asia? If you're just not really, *really* sure you have the chops to do it and need to spend more time "thinking it through"—guess what? Poof, it's gone, and the person who snatched it up might not have as much experience as you do! But one of you had the guts!

An opportunist understands that to make millions of dollars you have to go for it. That means being able to ignore insecurities and fears and pursue every opportunity available . . . each one pushing you up a little bit higher on the ladder of success. They want someone new to be the manager for the team of twelve employees. Yes, I'm there. They want a proposal. Consider it done. They want ideas for marketing a new product line—I'll sit down and sketch out ideas until I find one that will blow everyone's mind.

GO BIG OR FORGET IT

Two hours after my meeting with Winston Hendricks, Leah called me. "Someone is headed down to the building right now to fire the current sales director. We'd like you to start at 6 P.M. Does that work?" Well shit. I was on my way to the gym but: "Yes! Okay, great." Leah said she'd see me there. I won the project. But would I really have to get that tattoo? This was my first building, it was the first big job that helped me solidify my base as a broker to watch in 2009 and '10. It was the project that allowed me to showcase my unique strengths; Bloomberg News did a story on me. I was the youngest sales director ever! We transformed that building from a listing that wasn't getting any traffic to a very desirable place to live by rebranding it and creating a unique marketing campaign to draw in fresh buyers. I was showing New York City that when it came to real estate, I could be a giant! I was ready to take on more!

While I didn't really want to get a huge chest tattoo (it sounds so painful), the sentiment was basically the same. Given the opportunity I would be 100% in, I'd work tirelessly, I'd hire a great team, and I'd figure out how to get the job done. I'd live and breathe this project! Being a broker in New York City is cutthroat. If I didn't want to get toppled over by the competition, I needed to solidify my place—I'd have to grow deep roots and do everything I could do to stand strong. *I am the best broker in this damn forestverse, and I am going to stand strong like a fucking sequoia tree.* Sequoia trees are INSANE. They do not stop growing until the day they die, and they live for about 3,000 years. I want to be a seriously thick-skinned tree like this; their bark is three feet thick and it's *flame retardant*. They can't burn! Their branches are eight feet in diameter, so they spread out wide and take over TONS of space! My philosophy is go big or go home, so the sequoia is my spirit animal (after the aardvark, of course). Fast-forward to 2020, and my team is working on over fifty buildings in Manhattan and Brooklyn, and I've started my own company. I have since closed on over $4 billion in sales and I'm known for selling out new developments better than anyone else. But knock-it-out-of-the-universe-style success requires taking the knowledge and experience you've honed and using it to do more and earn more.

CONQUER

Real estate will always be where I earn most of my income, but all of the other branches I've pursued have also brought in more money that's growing like crazy. I give speeches all over the world, I started a brand new real estate network on YouTube called LISTED, the Sell It Like Serhant course has nearly 5,000 members, I have a deal with Chase Bank (where I deposited that first big commission check of $24,000) where I am THE face of real estate in their marketing, and I have a podcast called Big Money Energy (tune in please! you'll love it!).

All of these branches have become an integral part of my success, but I'm not solely dependent on any of them. A broken branch would hurt, sure—but I still have the strong base I'm operating from that allows me to identify new areas for growth. Next-level success requires conquering opportunities left and right—but do tell, Ryan, where exactly are all of these opportunities?

Start with that fantasy job or passion you haven't pursued because it seems so ridiculously unattainable!

Do What You Love (Kind of)
Sometimes I think whoever said, "Do what you love and the money will follow!" never worked a day in his life. In fact, he must not have earned a dollar in his lifetime.

If only earning money and being successful were that simple!

I haven't kept it a secret that being a real estate broker is NOT my dream job. I'd still be an actor if I had the skills of Daniel Day-Lewis, but I don't, and I know that. I'm self-aware enough to not try to make a living doing something I can't.

Coming to the realization that I was not going to make it as an actor was brutal! For whatever reason, I had to accept the fact that I was not going to become the next Tom Cruise. I would have been happy to be a B- or C-list actor, but I wasn't even going to be that. The harsh reality was, if I wanted to eat and pay my rent, I needed to get a REAL job.

But just because a dream doesn't play out like you wanted it to, doesn't mean that it DIES. My undying love for acting helped push me to work hard to get cast on *MDLNY* when that opportunity arose.

When I finally, miraculously, landed on TV after years of sad, failed attempts, I had to wonder—are there other ways to combine my true passion for performance with my day job in real estate, WHERE I AM ACTUALLY MAKING TOM CRUISE MONEY? How else can I tap into this?

Okay, I might not be playing Hamilton on Broadway, but thanks to my acting background I'm perfectly happy standing onstage and talking to thousands of people about how to improve their careers AND I LOVE IT. It energizes me and I feel a sense of connection with the audience—just like acting. And bonus, it pays a lot better than playing a bird in a subway performance of Alfred Hitchcock's *The Birds*.

The vlog is another area where I get to turn my love for performance into income-producing content for my real estate business. I've done an apartment tour in a bright-red, sleeveless suit with shorts, and I toured a house in Texas that had twenty-seven television sets while wearing a gigantic pink fur coat. Fine! So, I'm not playing Richard Gere's son in a movie, but I get to wear fun costumes while growing the most-followed real estate brand in the world!

This performance art works well for me, because I'm having fun and doing what I love while expanding my brand as a real estate agent, increasing my sphere of influence, gaining new subscribers, and ultimately making more money.

Just because the universe slammed the door in your face when it came to your big dream of being a fabulous fashion designer—Louis Vuitton Part 2—doesn't mean you can't find a different way to get it all in. Fuck you, Universe! Create a new way to do it. How can your passion become an extension of your business or an additional service to what you already offer?

No matter what field you work in, there are gaps in the marketplace! Guess what? Turns out people love crazy house tours where people display giant crystal-encrusted horse sculptures in their foyer and have enormous three-story closets! We get more followers with each crazy house I tour, and those followers turn into customers! When looking to branch out, think about how you can use your own passions and talents to pique interests, solve problems, and ultimately become a gigantic success story.

And suppose you're not creative. No problem! You just need to find a different way to break out of the mold as an opportunist.

You have to understand that there is also a whole stadium of other opportunists sitting in the bleachers, maybe with bigger money energy, who could be going for the same goals as you. Maybe they don't want to do a vlog, but they will still go for that million-dollar project. You've got to force yourself out of your comfort zone so that you aren't the last person sitting there in the bleachers while everyone else is out grabbing opportunities left and right.

GET OUT OF YOUR BUBBLE

When Emilia, Zena, and I move into our brownstone that we've been renovating for the past two years, I envision us all watching movies in cozy matching pajamas, or maybe I'll learn to make pancakes and start wearing an apron and operating a spatula. I can imagine the pride I'll feel when Zena rides her first bicycle up and down the street—and hopefully she'll inherit her parents' work ethic and operate a lucrative lemonade stand. That's the kind of life I see for myself. Pajamas! Carbs on Sundays! Juice for sale! And come Monday morning, Dad will put on his suit, straighten his tie, and head off to work for meetings. It's a wonderful life! But if I existed only in my bubble, where I am *most comfortable*, I would miss out on countless opportunities to branch out (how much seed capital do lemonade stands require, by the way?). I have to push myself out of my bubble.

Twice a month I schedule "growth work" in my calendar. These pockets of time are dedicated to attending events where I'll meet new interesting and creative people and be exposed to new ideas. I'll be the first person to admit that when I see "growth work" in my calendar, I want to throw up.

"Growth work" is the work that you don't want to do, so you reserve time in your calendar to do exactly that. Most of my growth work involves socializing, which basically means networking. However you want to classify it, I don't like to do it. It makes me nauseous to do it and I hate it so much, and that's exactly why I do it. It's the job—it's what I committed to doing, and because I'm an adult, I do what I tell myself I'm going to do!

But you know what I actually do like doing? PLAYING GAMES. My growth work involves making a social event into a *Grand Theft Auto* mission. I walk into an event with one simple goal: to meet *the smartest person in the room.* Boom. There he is. This serves as a perfect Jedi mind trick for me, because even though I'll just have finished a conversation with an investment banker who shared some brilliant ideas about mortgages, my mind is already reeling with possibilities—the truth is, how do I know he's the smartest person in the room? I DON'T! I'll push myself to investigate further, which means I'm forced to talk to someone else. I must find THE smartest person! Oh my God, this graphic designer is blowing my mind with creative ideas! Wow. *Is she the smartest?* I can't be sure! I'll force myself to talk to one more person. And finally, I'll meet another someone who specializes in online learning—what a smart guy! He gives me an idea: do an online class. Great idea! I'll do an online class! And just like that, I have a new venture to contribute to my millionaire plan.

Growth work always starts with me whining like a toddler who doesn't want to go to bed (because I really, really want to go home) and ends with me walking home thinking, *Oh my God, what if I had gone right home?* I left that party with a new way to think about investor loans, ideas about how to grow my media company—and the idea of an online class is amazing! Get out of your bubble to create more opportunities for yourself.

What's your bubble look like?

When I started doing growth work regularly, I couldn't believe how many new ideas I was generating. Some were admittedly ridiculous . . . no matter how much I love ice cream, I should not devote my energy to making calorie-free ice cream. Those ideas were tossed (although if someone invents that and it still tastes like ice cream and not cardboard cream, definitely let me know). Other ideas I wanted to explore right away, like bringing someone in-house to help me produce content. These were ideas I decided to ACT ON NOW. I'd bring the idea up to my team, start brainstorming and talking about how this branch might help us all grow. That's how opportunity works. You spot it and then execute to get the product out there and start making more money.

Other ideas, like the online class, got me very excited, but I knew I didn't have the time or staff to move forward with it *yet*. These ideas got placed in the future file labeled "Future Ryan."

The Future Ryan file is essentially a file of goals that I keep right on my desk, full of notes about things I want to accomplish but have to wait to proceed with until time and manpower are available. I visit my Future Ryan file every month, adding to it, looking through the ideas to see if any of them have become viable yet.

Growth work has led to the writing of this book! If I hadn't been on *MDLNY*, I wouldn't have had the opportunity to do the show *Sell It Like Serhant*, which led to the opportunity to do a master class for real estate brokers in New York City. Talking in front of all those successful brokers showed me that—Wow, I have something to say! I realized at that moment I had gained enough knowledge to put a book together.

None of this would have happened if on my way to do growth work I had let myself take the easy way out and said, "Oh, I'm doing great. I'm making money, I'll just give myself a break and go home and watch Netflix." Netflix is great, but it's not going to help you discover lucrative new opportunities to help you make millions. Get out of your bubble and go grow!

Opportunists are constantly looking for growth. We feed off growth. We take each opportunity and squeeze it for everything it's worth.

Opportunists have Big Money Energy because they are always listening closely for the next fix. They go to bed smiling when a new idea arises because they have a new opportunity to jump onto first thing in the morning.

NO THANK YOU

After my experience selling my first building I knew one thing: I wanted to focus on the Big FO (not FU!). The Big FO may sound like a cuisine, but it really stands for "future opportunities."

While I wish there wasn't a limit to what a single human can accomplish, there is. I'm limited in what I can accomplish today, but not next year or next week. Time gives me more stamina. If you're anything like me, the idea of turning down work makes you want to throw up. But when you're expanding, you need to grab on to opportunities that also buy you time into the future. There are opportunities for right now—renting an apartment, opening a yoga studio on the side—and then there's the Big FO. We've all operated in the now, and that's fine! But in order to surge ahead and make millions, you need to graduate to the bigger goals—selling and flipping homes, owning a chain of yoga studios, you name it! After being a sales director of an entire building, I was hungry for more FO. I started asking myself three questions before I took on any project, to evaluate if it would lead to more FO:

How many minutes is this costing me? By now you've learned that I am passionately protective of my minutes. Minutes are as valuable as gold! So it's important to analyze if the minutes spent are worth the amount of potential income. A thousand minutes for $1,000 commission or profit is a clear *no thank you.* The more minutes, the more money I have to make. And will this deplete my minutes? If a project presents complications from the very beginning, I need to analyze if the minutes spent are worth the amount of potential income. If it's not worth it, pass it off to someone junior on your team.

Is there a visible path to FO? Just to make the equation slightly more complicated, a project that would require thousands of minutes to make a moderate commission SEEMS like a clear *no thank you.* But if the project involves working with a developer who I KNOW has many more, bigger projects in the pipeline, then the math might work in favor of taking the job.

Will I make invaluable connections? An old, dusty brownstone that hasn't been modernized can be hard to sell. People love sleek new kitchens! No one wants dumbwaiters! They're creepy. A project like this could suck up thousands of my minutes for one sale. But hold the phone; if I get a good price for this brownstone, I'll have planted the seed that I can get a great price for other homes on the block. This could lead to other listings from neighbors whose homes I could sell for huge amounts of money. The referrals this could bring are solid FOs, so this is a YES.

As you're branching out, analyze the situation to the best of your ability—how much time will it take? What's the payoff? Is that worth the hard work it will take? Will putting in the work NOW bring me much larger opportunities in the FUTURE? If your main focus is currently growing branches, get comfortable holding out for more FO and leaving those smaller, lower-paying, energy-sucking jobs for someone else.

DON'T PLAY IT SAFE

When I first moved to New York and lived in Koreatown, the first thing I'd see in the morning was the wall on the other side of my bed. A grungy, sort of cigarette-smoke-colored wall with nothing on it. It's like I opened my eyes every morning and was confronted with my total lack of abundance in the form of a depressing, gross wall. If that wall could talk it would have said, "Good morning, Ryan, welcome to another day in your sucky life." This was not an experience I wanted to repeat every morning for the rest of my life. I started to visualize something better. I'd wake up, and before opening my eyes I'd imagine I lived in a penthouse apartment. In my mind that apartment was in SoHo, a neighborhood I loved. My bedroom would have actual walls and a door (I was living in a studio), and when I woke up, I'd have a view of the city outside of my window with my own private terrace. I'd imagine myself getting up and taking a shower in a beautiful marble bathroom—maybe it would have a walk-in rain shower like the nicer apartments in New York City did, with a hand wand. And the best part is I wouldn't have to literally wait in line to use said bathroom because it was MY OWN DAMN BATHROOM. The rest of my apartment would be tastefully decorated with good furniture . . . the walls would not be the color of death and there would be actual art hanging on them.

It would take a few years, but I got that penthouse in SoHo and it's everything I imagined it would be. I don't think lying in bed and envisioning your dream life is like a magic formula for making what you want appear, but I do believe that thinking about your dream life inspires you to go out into the world and work harder to earn more. Focusing on what you really, *really* want can push you to take risks. Maybe thinking about how great it would feel to drive a car that isn't falling apart will push you to call that new contact you made last week. You don't want roommates anymore? Then it's time to really push for that promotion so you can earn more and afford the apartment that makes your heart sing. You want to wake up excited about the satisfying work you're doing to save the world? Then go out there and finally get the job that makes you WANT TO GET UP AND GO TO WORK.

Take time every day to think about what bigger dreams and bigger earnings can bring you. A luxurious European vacation or paying for college—how awesome to picture your kids in their caps and gowns walking across a stage on graduation day! What a great motivator! Maybe you imagine paying off all of that credit card debt, and you think about lying in the park without a care in the world before the first of every month. If you want to open your own business, imagine what it would be like to leave your house and walk into your very own company! Knowing that the options are limitless and allowing yourself to WANT IT ALL will open you up to doing more, exploring new opportunities, and getting creative about how to make it happen. I'm writing this from the dining room table in my penthouse apartment, and I wouldn't be here if I woke up every morning, saw that gross wall and thought, *Sure, this is enough for me.* Aim higher! And guess what? Once you get what you want, your dreams will change and you'll have something new to aim for. As I'm typing this, I'm also renovating my new 8,000-square-foot Brooklyn brownstone—the largest single-family home in Boerum Hill, a very fancy neighborhood in Brooklyn. I dreamt it too. I got it.

If you want to earn more, don't play it safe. Safe is fine. Safe will get you an average life, an average income, and alllllllll of the average things that come along with it. You are not average! What can you do to break out of your safe zone and start earning more? Think about the craziest ideas you ever had—are they really that crazy? What's holding you back? Open yourself up to new possibilities, toss some of those safety precautions aside, and just take a risk! Say goodbye to "average" forever and see what you can do when you just take a risk.

BIG MONEY ENERGY

MANTRA #3

I know how badly you want your dream to come true, and that's why you can't let negative energy and self-doubt weigh you down. You must exude positivity to succeed.

I AM UPBEAT

I AM EXPANSIVE

I RADIATE SUCCESS

I HAVE BIG MONEY ENERGY

THE BLUEPRINT: POSITIVE ENERGY

The way we view the world has such an enormous impact on the level of success we can experience. Chances are, if you think everything sucks—everything is going to continue sucking. And you are not putting yourself in a place to succeed if you are operating from such a negative mindset. Opening up your positive energy takes work, but it's so worth it! When I learned to shed my habit of finding the negative in any situation, my life opened up to me. I was finding solutions when it seemed like there were none; I was finding opportunities I thought would never be available to me. I connected with other people who were positive and also wanted to aim high and do huge things with their life. The power to do this is in you; let yourself see what you can achieve when you turn up the volume on your positive energy.

STEP ONE: The Positive/Negative Challenge
Take a few minutes to jot down positive and negative experiences throughout the day to train your brain to operate on the bright side. Spoiler alert—the positive side should be longer!

STEP TWO: Structure, Plan, Outlast
- **Create a superstructure** to protect your success.
- **Build your road map** to future opportunities.
- **Maintain momentum** to beat your competition.

STEP THREE: Schedule Growth Time
Get out of your bubble to meet different people and learn new things.

CHAPTER 13

WHY NOT ME?

I know the seven days of the week, and I can tell you that "someday" isn't a real day. I don't ever want to be the old man who thinks, "I should have."

Whenever Yuriy picks me up from the airport and drives me back to Manhattan after a speaking gig, we pass by Calvary Cemetery, the largest cemetery in New York City. Calvary Cemetery is the final resting place for 3 MILLION PEOPLE.

The gravestones seem to stretch out for miles, with the city skyline highlighted in the background (as a final resting place, it's some prime real estate—that view!).

As we drive past, I can't help but wonder, How many of these people said at some point in their lives, "I have a really great idea!" How many acted on them? Did thousands of these people get buried here and say they'd do it *someday*?

Ideas aren't any good unless you act on them. And that's why you don't need to hate on opportunists or people with an accelerated path. Let their drive to get things done inspire you! Let their ability to grab on to opportunities and make things happen motivate you to succeed on a higher level and push you to keep growing.

I'm proud to know that I can keep growing in new directions. I still think about what I said to myself when I was surrounded by countless other brokers in the Gotham Hotel who were all going after the same opportunity I was—*why not me*? I never tattooed the address of my first building on my chest, and while I don't have any plans for a tattoo, if I got one I think I'd go in a different direction: WHY NOT ME?

I didn't know it when I was a kid in my mid-twenties, awkward in my dorky clothes and insanely nervous around clients, but my success has been shaped by the idea "why not me?" If it wasn't me it was going to be someone else! That question gave me the power to grab on to what I wanted; it helped me understand that I had just as much right to big success as anyone else. As you start putting the pieces of your extraordinary life together, there's going to be moments where you feel stuck—when the task before you feels insurmountable. That's okay. You're not the first person to feel that way; you aren't the first person who has considered giving up as they pursue their dreams. Just keep going forward because, why not you? I AM HERE TO TELL YOU THAT YOU'RE READY! If you don't believe me (yet) consider the following:

PROOF YOU'RE READY FOR MORE

You've Reached Expert Status
If people are calling you for your take on what *you think*—the next big development, your thoughts on what the next new digital marketing application will look like, congratu-

lations! You're an expert and a thought leader. You're the go-to person for start-ups, issues regarding urban planning in your town? THAT MEANS YOU'RE AN EXPERT. You know what you're doing and it's a clear sign that you're ready to handle more.

You Consistently Overdeliver

You may have reached a place in your career where the nuts and bolts of what you do are getting easier. Now, when you're hired to do an online marketing campaign, you're also able to use all of your savviness to help your clients place op-eds in major newspapers! That's an impressive skill, and it's also going above and beyond. If you're consistently able to push the envelope for your clients and customers, you're ready for more. Go for it!

Your Team Is in Place

Your branding company has been consistently growing for a while and you've hired great people. Your team is working well together, there's collaboration on projects, and you have strong systems in place.

The workload is flowing steadily, and the manpower is there—what are you waiting for? Branch out!

Everything I have done in my life, from going on reality TV to building my own company to creating a podcast, has been shaped by the fact that when my life and career felt as tumultuous as a level-four rapid, I didn't stop paddling. If you have a great idea, whether it's to expand your company, build a new business from scratch, or monetize your side hustle—galvanize yourself to just get in that boat and start paddling. Just keep moving down the river, because your ideas deserve to be heard, you deserve to be seen, you deserve to live a life that you love, just like anyone else.

You might start out in gentle waters; the river is clear and you can see any hazards that are headed towards you . . . but then you're going to experience those irregular waves that rock your confidence. You have to keep paddling to stay afloat, and you'll be okay. Next you could hit narrow channels that are hard to maneuver through. You might hit waters so violent you can get tossed right out of your boat. But when that happens, GET BACK IN. The river is rough, but eventually you'll gain the strength you need to move forward with confidence. And guess what? Just when you think you're past the rough waters, surprise! That's when the river dumps you right into the ocean where the waves are bigger than anything you've experienced. But you'll be fine—because you are going to swim right through those waves. You've proved your worth on the river, and you can cut through ALL of this until you land where you want to be.

If you don't keep paddling, if you decide to abandon your boat and crawl onto the banks, that's fine—but there is someone else who is waiting anxiously behind you to get in your seat. If not you, it's going to be someone else! So, why not you?

You need to fully believe that you have just as much right to big success as anyone else. As you start putting the pieces of your extraordinary life together, there's going to be moments where you feel stuck, when the task before you feels INSURMOUNTABLE. That's okay; you're not the first person to feel that way; you aren't the first person who has considered giving up as they pursue their dreams. Just stay in the boat, just keep paddling and moving yourself down the river because, why not you? You are going to be bold and keep going because YES, YOU! Never forget that success is 100% yours for the taking! Let's see how far your BIG MONEY ENERGY takes you.

ACKNOWLEDGMENTS

Thank you to my wife, Emilia, for encouraging me to go bigger with every move I make. You push me because you know that's when I do my best work, and even though I make angry faces, deep down I love you for it. Heart emoji.

To my parents for giving me energy from birth. Without your constant advice (which I sometimes listen to) I'm not sure where I would be today.

To all of the dreamers, thinkers, creators, innovators, and entrepreneurs at SERHANT., selling more real estate than anyone else with me every day.

To Paula Balzer Vitale, who again has helped take what I have in my head and turn it into something the world can understand.

Thank you to Brandi Bowles and Natasha Bolouki at United Talent Agency.

And to everyone at Hachette for believing in me AGAIN: my editor, Krishan Trotman, Carrie Napolitano, Mary Ann Naples, Michelle Aielli, Michael Barrs, Sarah Falter, Monica Oluwek, Christine Marra, Gray Cutler, and the Hachette Book Group sales force.

And to all of YOU, my *Big Money Energy* followers. You inspire the hell out of me with your courage to do more. What you want is just around the bend! Keep paddling, and I will see you there.